"One of the best books written about the Law of Attraction—really a masterpiece."

"Awesome read!!! I've spent the last few years reading all the books written about the Law of Attraction and this gem of a book fills in all the gaps that so many of the others leave out. It's a simple read—took me a few hours, but don't underestimate its simplicity. The author's fascination with the Law of Attraction, quantum field and intention to manifestation principle really comes through.

"This author is intelligent and extremely thorough. I highly recommend this book and am grateful to the author for producing this masterpiece. And yes, it really is a masterpiece. If you're practicing the principles of the Law of Attraction and not getting the results you want, I can tell you why right now. It's because you haven't read this book!!! — D. Margolis, New York, NY

"I've read this book 4 times — truly powerful!"

"I've been studying the Law of Attraction for about a year, and when I encountered *The Greatest Manifestation Principle in the World,* it made so much sense and I truly enjoyed reading it — and I've read it 4 times in the last few weeks. Upon looking back on the successes of my life, I find that the greatest manifestation principle which this book talks about WAS the underlying factor.

"I started life as an orphan and surmounted much in my life. I started a company, DC Group, with $5 in my pocket and 1 employee (myself) and it has become a multimillion-dollar nationwide business poised to double in size next year. I think my success owes itself to the fact that I touch a lot of people and endeavor to live my life the way the book teaches readers how. I've also realized that most Law of Attraction practices, spiritual work, and rituals such as affirmations, visualization, positive thoughts and feelings are only truly powerful when infused with the greatest manifestation principle. I've cured lifelong illnesses and traumas and created wellness in my life as a result." — Jonathan Frank., CEO, DC Group, Inc., Minneapolis, Minnesota

"This profound book blew me away ... it's divinely inspired!"

"I have read a lot of material about the Law of Attraction. I've even taken classes to become a Law of Attraction practitioner. And yet I still learned so much from *The Greatest Manifestation Principle in the World*. I could not put it down. I was so blown away by this profound book! It is so well written that I'm convinced it's divinely inspired. It is elegant in its simplicity, and it addresses the 'elephant in the room,' namely what everyone is thinking, but no one is bold enough to say out loud — "I believe in the Law of *Attraction, I've been using it, but it's just not working for me!'*

"This book showed me how LOA results are related to motive. I've used LOA so many times with almost zero results, but I saw it work for me BIG TIME in four separate instances in my life. In those four times, the spectacular results were fueled by the "greatest manifestation principle" of which this book speaks. I'm convinced that LOA works when we are in alignment with that principle. It can't help but work because the resulting state of being is our true nature." — Mary Beth Spann Mank, Amazon Verified Purchaser of *The Greatest Manifestation Principle* book

"Absolutely Phenomenal"

"Wow! This book is absolutely phenomenal! It's about time someone had the courage to go against the contemporary teachings and dispel myths that are currently being taught by the Law of Attraction gurus. The first couple of chapters ... are actually what everyone "must know" about this Law and why so many are failing miserably when attempting to apply it. Carnelian did an excellent job presenting the information, including the missing secret, in an easy to read, logical, and simple to follow format. I can probably write a novella review here but I will sum it up by saying that **of all the courses, books, audios, and conversations I had regarding this topic, it is by**

far the best I ever encountered. If you have been failing miserably in manifesting your desires, then you need this book!" — Alex Rosmondo, Amazon Verified Purchaser of *The Greatest Manifestation Principle* book

"The fundamental cornerstone of co-creation and manifestation!"

"I'm one of those who's always been convinced that people who believe in the Law of Attraction are full of delusion. It doesn't take a genius to realize that those that follow the Law of Attraction and send out positive thoughts to the universe are only fooling themselves. I've personally never met one single person who's achieved what they positively focused on — even when they did it consistently and faithfully. What disgusts me even more are those so-called Law of Attraction 'gurus' that have taken advantage of the Law of Attraction craze by selling super-expensive courses, memberships to Secret Coaching Clubs, seminars and workshops. They jump up and down and pump you up by saying how great the Law of Attraction is — and yet most of them are as poor as a mouse, and have rarely manifested their own dreams of abundance. I was just about fed up with all the nonsense when I came upon a jewel of a book titled The Greatest Manifestation Principle in the World. Talk about life-changing! This book really gets to the heart of the matter — and delves into the fundamental cornerstone of co-creation and manifestation. Then, it gives a simple exercise that takes only a few minutes to do, and enables you to practice the principle in your daily life. The book says, 'The outcome you get may be different from what you had in mind, but it will be infinitely better than that which you desired.' This has been true in my experience, and looking back over my life, I've discovered that I've been successful whenever I practiced this principle, and unsuccessful (or not as successful as I'd like to be) when I did not practice the principle. I think this book contains the real SECRET that every human being should live by. Truly life-changing!" — Melanie Anton, Santa Barbara, California

"It works every time without fail !!!"

"Carnelian Sage puts her finger on several of the flaws in Law of Attraction teaching that have bothered me for some time, when she reveals the 5 myths and dangers behind the so-called Law of Attraction. More importantly, however, she reveals the true spiritual principle that does work every time without fail. The Love's Pathway exercise is phenomenal. Already I have seen positive effects of my doing this exercise in my relationship with my teenage son. This little book needs to be read and digested by everyone who has read *The Secret* and other Law of Attraction books, as both a corrective and a crucial supplement." — Diane Eble, Book Publishing Coach, www.WordsToProfit. com, Winfield, IL

"Mind blown!"

"If you never pick up and read another book in your entire life, read this one first! This book is not only very well written, but the theme of the book creates an awareness in you that few people completely understand or have mastered up until now. This book delivers and is very satisfying and very instrumental in making powerful mind shifts to those who read it and apply it's beautiful teachings and lessons." — Elizabeth, Amazon Verified Purchaser of *The Greatest Manifestation Principle* book

"A must-have and a must-read book"

"When I was first introduced to *The Greatest Manifestation Principle in the World,* I was a bit skeptical. I thought at first the author was someone who possibly was trying to piggy-back off of the success of *The Secret.* But I was intrigued enough to start reading the first chapter of this so-called 'missing secret' book. I must admit I walked in as a skeptic but walked out a true believer. I found myself personally agreeing with a lot of the different key points and in the end actually seeing what was missing in making a true connection with how the Law of Attraction is supposed to work and how it really works. Newfound light and newfound spirit is what I personally received from this amazing book. It not only assisted me in manifestation but it also assisted me in so many other parts of my personal life. A must- have, a must-read, and a must for anyone who really wants to experience change and not just another empty level of self-help." — Everett N., Los Angeles, CA

"Will read this little treasure over and over ..."

"This little book is the most honest and simple book on manifesting that I've read since this movement began. After reading it, I felt that I had finally come to the truth of the matter and would not need to read another book on this subject. My search is finally over. I found this little treasure and will read it over and over until my subconscious mind finally gets it." — Yves, Amazon Verified Purchaser of *The Greatest Manifestation Principle* book

"An inspiring book that will stun you!"

"I've long been a seeker of deeper spiritual wisdom. I found quantum physics fascinating, and the Law of Attraction compelling, but I knew deep inside that there was something missing that wasn't enabling me to manifest my heart's desires. *The Greatest Manifestation Principle in the World* offered a refreshing approach to the Law of Attraction, and I was quickly entranced by the powerful spiritual concepts it contained. Among the things I learned from reading the book was how the author, Carnelian Sage, suffered through financial struggles and a 4-year career 'meltdown' — even while practicing everything she had previously learned about the Law of Attraction. It was through her time of despair that she accidentally discovered `the greatest manifestation principle in the world' and she offered compelling evidence that it, indeed, was the secret to entering the realm of miracles. Within the past 5 months of putting this principle into practice myself, I've already seen desires manifesting into existence in my life. I can't recommend this wonderful little book enough! You'll be inspired at a level that will stun you. It reveals a truth, and a technique for rediscovering that truth for your life. You'll smile over its simplicity, and be an important step closer to the `knowing' you desire, the `knowing' that connects ALL of us. THIS, my friend, is what really works!" — Tim G., Trumbull, Connecticut

"Finally ... a manifestation book without the Fairy Godmother approach! I highly recommend it."

"I read *The Greatest Manifestation Principle in the World* last night in one sitting. I couldn't put it down. Having watched The Secret video and read books about turning thoughts into things, all the way back to Napoleon Hill's *Think and Grow Rich,* I'm fairly familiar with the subject of manifestation, although I must admit I have not researched it to the degree that Carnelian Sage has. Like the author, I have found myself uncomfortable with the Fairy Godmother approach to manifestation that the other books have suggested. I found this book to be refreshing because, among other things, it points to divinity (or God) as the actual source of all things, and we human beings are co-creators.

"Most specifically, I thoroughly enjoyed the aspect that I find often missing in so many of the other manifestation books, namely the idea of virtue. Although the author did not mention the word specifically, she alluded to it in many ways. After having practiced focusing on material things so often in the past, I became tired of it because what I really wanted had less to do with money and materialistic ideals and more to do with things I deeply love — like people and God. I agree wholeheartedly with the concept presented in the book, which says that only when we step outside ourselves and our selfish interests do we really manifest our heart's desires and become truly blessed. I highly recommend this book!" — Bob Grant, Acworth, Georgia

"I've read them all and this one is the best!"

"I have read every author imaginable when it comes to manifestation even *'The Secret'*. I have also traveled the world and have opened my mind & heart completely to a spiritual life but still something has been missing. For 20 years I have been on a path of growth and enlightenment and if there is a course, author or practice that helps, I have tried it! Recently I started my own company, The 180 Degree Life, where the focus is on positive change and this little book has helped me in more ways than I can write here. In a materialistic world we get caught up in our egos and it is difficult to understand when something goes wrong in our lives when we are doing all the right things. I read one review that said this book was like *The Secret* but with a spiritual spin. I actually believe this book is the opposite of The Secret as it requires you to transcend your ego where *The Secret* is actually asking you to engage it by controlling your thoughts. I have studied meditation and non-attachment is the way to go for overall health and happiness. Once the ego is in its right place and our hearts are leading the way, nothing can stop us. Unfortunately, books like The Secret are a dead end, where this one is the path and the way to true fulfillment. I will read this book over and over again. Just in a short time it has made a profound difference. My husband and my closest friends have all seen a change in me. A shift toward a calmer and more loving presence." — Lyn Patrick, Verified Amazon Purchaser of *The Greatest Manifestation Principle* book

"Truly Amazing!"

"The author is a person of deep spiritual awareness. She was able to transcend the multitude of other authors involved in their writings concerning the levels of consciousness. I love this book because of the simplicity in which the author presents and explains the steps involved in attaining the goal of coupling the law of attraction with the "hidden truth" which will then allow one to connect to the "encrgy field" which enables one to remove the obstacles (wrong beliefs etc...) into the awareness of love's presence within one's self... "Truly Amazing!" — Thomas C. Breggia, Amazon Verified Purchaser of *The Greatest Manifestation Principle* book

"Makes Your Life Richer and More Beautiful"

"The Law of Attraction finally makes sense. Carnelian Sage's insights in *The Greatest Manifestation Principle in the World* give meaning and control to a practice that was formless and unpredictable. I've always wanted to believe in the Law of Attraction, and occasionally The Law has seemed to work for me. After reading *The Greatest Manifestation Principle in the World,* I understand why. Even if you've read the other books, watched the DVD, and followed the TV shows, you need to read this book. If you don't believe in the Law of Attraction, Sage's beautifully written book still suggests ways to make your life richer and more beautiful. The Love's Pathway exercise alone makes the book a must-have." — Rebecca Nelson, Chicago, Illinois

"The best book I've read about the Law of Attraction"

"I'm positively stoked! I read this slim volume, *The Greatest Manifestation Principle in the World,* in one evening, and was convinced this MUST be the ultimate secret to life. I'm also convinced that when people learn how to apply the manifestation principle in their day-to-day existence, it has a transforming effect on their life and the lives of those around them. And to think it is such an obvious principle, just waiting to be discovered. Just goes to show that we humans like to complicate things that are meant to be simple—and we go off searching for the magic fairy dust when the real magic is within us all along! This is the best book I've read about the Law of Attraction. I know without a doubt it will help me get what I really want in life." — Avery Tierney, Detroit, Michigan

"A deeply profound and insightful jewel of a book!"

"The Greatest Manifestation Principle in the World is a must-read for anyone who has been misled by The Secret DVD and book. This beautifully written, deeply profound and insightful jewel of a book reveals the missing information heretofore unexplained about the Law of Attraction. It's not only a real page turner, but it's a life-changing book that I intend to read all the time for inspiration. You'll want to buy a copy for everyone you love! — Angela I., Long Island City, NY

"This book is by far the BEST manifestation book ... this is the missing piece"

"I have read so many other manifestation books, *'The Secret,' 'Think and Grow Rich,'* Florence Scovill Schinn and other authors — and this book is by far the best. It explains in easy to use ways exactly how to connect to the universe and FEEL what it is we want to help us bring it into our lives. I also felt this was the missing piece, feeling love then gratitude and letting it surround you and encompass your life, both internally and externally. I highly recommend this book to anyone — it is far superior and gives us what the others miss." — J. Anton, Desert Hot Springs, California

"Rocked My World!"

The Greatest Manifestation Principle in the World rocked my world! I had already experienced some of those teachings, from Spirit. Reading them, and the way you put them into words, was very profound. Yes, Love is everything!!!" — Catherine W., Springville, Utah

"Truly amazing!"

"I've been a law-of-attraction aficionado for some time now — but *The Greatest Manifestation Principle in the World* reveals truths that are truly amazing. This is a life-changing book!" — Dominique D., Diamond Bar, California

"I think I've finally found the real deal!"

"I've spent the last 11 years trying to 'attract' my dreams by practicing the Law of Attraction — and I found myself still stuck in a dead-end job as a limo driver, and not getting any breaks in my acting career. I watched *The Secret* DVD summer of last year, and my enthusiasm for the Law of Attraction was rekindled, even though the DVD didn't teach me anything I didn't already know.

"After going gung-ho for several months with no results, I began to wonder whether I was just kidding myself by believing in all this Law of Attraction mumbo-jumbo. Then, I received an e-mail offering an advance copy of *The Greatest Manifestation Principle in the World,* and I said to myself, 'I'm going to try this one last thing before giving up on the Law of Attraction forever.' Before I was halfway through the book, I already began to see circumstances in my life change for the better. When I finished reading the book in 5 days' time and started practicing the manifestation principle daily, Whoa! I was shocked at how quickly my life turned around.

"I received a call from a casting agent, who cast me in a co-starring role in a major motion picture that will start shooting in a few months. The girl I've been in love with for 2 years, who previously wouldn't reciprocate my affection, suddenly called me out of the blue, telling me she's matured enough to be my girl! In addition, people began to show up in my life that believed in me and were willing to help me take my acting career where I want it to go. I wondered if this was merely a coincidence. Well, I'm not gonna question this principle because it's the only thing about the Law of Attraction that has actually helped me attract good things to myself. I can't wait to see what else I can attract into my life by simply practicing this manifestation principle. I think I've finally found the real deal!" — M. Petersen., Studio City, California

"My relationships have deepened, and the guy I'm dating wants to marry me"

"I read *Excuse Me Your Life is Waiting* in early 2006 and it got me really excited about the Law of Attraction. I began practicing the good 'feeeeeelings' that the author suggested. Then, I came upon The Secret DVD a couple of months later and I got even more excited after hearing the wonderful things that have happened to the 'master teachers' who spoke on the DVD — one of them got a million-dollar dream house, another person healed herself of cancer, another went from broke to rich, etc.

"I began practicing the Law of Attraction faithfully for one solid year, and I have yet to manifest more than just the handful of good parking spaces that I've attracted thus far! Just when I began to think this Law of Attraction thing was just one big bogus propaganda, I received a review copy of *The Greatest Manifestation Principle in the World*. Wow, did it ever spin my head around! I realized there was a missing ingredient in my practice of the Law of Attraction, and when I started adding that missing ingredient, I was amazed at the results.

"I'm a 37-year-old single woman who's been seeking to have an enduring relationship with a man, and hopefully get married before I turn 40. As soon as I started practicing the manifestation principle, I began meeting several interesting eligible bachelors who, surprisingly, were also romantically interested in me. One of them, whom I've gone on 5 dates with, turned out to be a marriage-minded man who's been hinting to me that he wishes to marry me one day! I've been dating for over 20 years and I've NEVER come this close to possibly receiving a marriage proposal. I'm crossing my fingers!

"I find that the more I practice the manifestation principle, the more in love with me this guy seems to be. I think I send out some kind of good vibes when I practice the principle, and I'm lovin' it! My girlfriends have commented that they started to notice some 'alluring' quality about me — and my relationships with both women and men have deepened. I know it has everything to do with my practice of the principle. I can honestly say that with daily practice of the 5-minute exercise taught in the book, I'm becoming a much better person — more caring and generous — unlike the self-absorbed person I used to be before. I've recommended this book to everyone I know!" — Susan K., Vancouver, Washington

"All aspects of my life — finances, career and love life — are getting better!"

"I used to be really skeptical about anything that had to do with the Law of Attraction. I've been into positive thinking for several years, and I felt that those teaching the Law of Attraction are just pretty much saying the same old things that positive thinkers have been saying for over 20 years. While positive thinking has its advantages and has improved my outlook in life, it certainly has rarely changed my circumstances. It just made me a more optimistic person. So when I started reading the new slew of books about the Law of Attraction that have come out in the last few years, I remained skeptical — until someone at work passed on a galley copy of *The Greatest Manifestation Principle in the World* to me. Finally, here's a book that tells it like it is — and goes well beyond positive thinking. It removes all the 'woowoo' magic dust that seems to predominate all the other books on the subject. I've only had this book for 3 weeks, and yet I've already seen positive changes in me and in my circumstances. It seems that all aspects of my life — from my finances to my career and my love life — are getting better, and opportunities for growth and advancement are suddenly plentiful." — T. Milliken, St. Paul, Minnesota

The Greatest

Manifestation Principle in the World

How Quantum Physics and Spirituality Can Enable You to Manifest Your Best Life

SECOND EDITION

Carnelian Sage

 Think-Outside-the-Book, Inc.

ISBN 978-0-9896781-3-1

Publisher:

 Think-Outside-the-Book, Inc.

8465 W. Sahara Avenue, Ste. 111-497
Summerlin, Nevada 89117
www.GreatestManifestationPrinciple.com

Contents

AUTHOR'S INTRODUCTION TO THE SECOND
EDITION 1

Chapter 1
The Field of Infinite Potentiality 15

Chapter 2
The Science Behind Manifestation 31

Chapter 3
To Love is to Live 57

Chapter 4
Entering the Realm of Miracles 81

Chapter 5
How to Infuse Your Life with the Greatest
Manifestation Principle 101

APPENDIX 115

AUTHOR'S INTRODUCTION TO THE SECOND EDITION

When I wrote the first edition of *The Greatest Manifestation Principle in the World* in 2007, the concept called the "law of attraction" had just started gaining massive popularity. Millions of people were *seduced* by the lure of the law of attraction and its promise of manifesting wealth, health and all the good things in life. Over the past decade, the law of attraction's appeal seems to have dimmed considerably—especially when most people discovered for themselves that practicing it yielded disappointing—or even harmful—results.

People failed to manifest anything except the most trivial wishes when they followed the then-prevailing "best practices" taught by law of attraction teachers. That's the original reason why I wrote the first edition of this book. The book gained a loyal following of tens of thousands of people—even though it preached a "missing secret" that was contrary to law of attraction principles. This book corrected the inaccuracies, identified the hidden dangers, and dispelled the myths surrounding the law of attraction. More importantly, it shed light on the most powerful manifestation principle that no one was talking about— one which, when practiced, enabled one to enter the realm of miracles where one's desires can and <u>must</u> necessarily manifest into existence.

The frenzy surrounding the law of attraction—followed by the resulting disenchantment experienced by so many people—devalued the law of attraction somewhat and caused many people to overlook the profound truths inherent in the practice of *true manifestation.*

I define manifestation as the metaphysical art of consciously transmuting thoughts and desires into reality. It's a frontier that goes far beyond the scope of the law of attraction—one which fuses together the seemingly disparate domains of *quantum physics and spirituality.* Just as the medieval science of alchemy transmuted base metals into gold, the greatest manifestation principle has the power to transform your life in mysterious ways that defy explanation. The phenomenon is called **spiritual alchemy**, whereby a single profound truth can turn your innermost desires from their unformed potentiality into physical existence.

No, it's not magic or wizardry, which is how the law of attraction has been portrayed. Manifestation is a brilliant synthesis of consciousness-based science and spirituality. The synergy of the two disciplines yields mind-boggling outcomes that transcend ordinary levels of understanding.

In the past 13 years, I have received countless e-mails and letters from readers reporting remarkable stories of desires manifesting into reality through the use of the greatest manifestation principle revealed in this book.

A letter that I found particularly gratifying and humbling at the same time was from a spiritually-minded man named Marcus, who had read practically all the books on manifestation available. It was his custom to "calibrate" each of the books he read using the Map of Consciousness® developed by the late David Hawkins, MD, PhD. Dr. Hawkins had conducted a 29-year study that demonstrated that the human body becomes stronger or weaker depending on a person's mental state, and this research was based on the well-established science of Applied Kinesiology. The Map of Consciousness® is a numerical scale whereby one can measure positive from negative, power from force, and truth from falsehood.

The scale goes from 1 to 1,000—with 1 being the lowest level of truth and consciousness and 1,000 being the highest level. Marcus calibrated *The Greatest Manifestation Principle in the World* using Applied Kinesiology, and reported his findings, saying the book measured at level 1,000 on the Map of Consciousness® —the highest of any book he had ever read. That meant that this book is at the highest level of truth and consciousness. *(The Map of Consciousness® is explained in more detail on page 38.)*

Manifestation is both a science and a spiritual precept that *transcends religion*—although some of the spiritual truths inherent in the practice of the greatest manifestation principle resemble those taught in certain spiritual ideologies. A Christian reader named Naomi wrote, *"Next to the Holy Bible, this is the most valuable book I've ever read."* Another reader named Daphne sent me a check representing 10% of her income, and said it was her *tithe* for the month that she was giving to me (instead of her church) as her way of helping spread the uplifting doctrine presented in the book. The important takeaway to all this is that the greatest manifestation principle is based on a simple yet profound universal truth that merges seamlessly with any religious beliefs one might embrace. You may find that it could even enhance your current spiritual practices—and become the blueprint for **answered prayer**.

The phenomenal results that the greatest manifestation principle has materialized in my own life have proven the power of the principle beyond any doubt—and similar outcomes are within reach of anyone who abides by its central profound truth. I humbly share with you my personal story, which might seem incredible to anyone who hears it, but nonetheless, it is entirely true and verifiable.

When I turned 52, I realized to my great dismay that my life up to that point was quite unremarkable. I didn't have a real career because I had spent the last 28 years hopping from one job to another in industries that were all dissimilar. I had a total of 21 jobs, never spending more than 2 years in any one of them—and at the end of the day, I found that I had learned very little and mastered nothing. I managed to always earn an above-average salary but spent a great deal of time trying to convince people that I was more prosperous than I really was. In reality, I was a low net-worth individual (compared to other people my age). I was still renting and didn't own any real property. In fact, I was the only one among my 7 siblings who didn't yet own a single-family house, a townhouse or a condo. My 16-year marriage had ended in divorce, and I was flitting from one unfulfilling relationship to the next. If anyone was ever in greater need of manifesting their desires into reality, it was me.

The worst part was, I didn't know how to get myself out of the rut I had made of my life.

In 2006, I bought all the law of attraction books I could get my hands on, and went full-speed in my effort to change my life for the better—all to no avail. Just like everyone else I knew who had tried to practice the law of attraction, I failed to manifest anything of real value—no matter how hard I tried.

It was in mid-2007 that I stumbled upon the "greatest manifestation principle" from a spiritual leader (see page 28), which later became the subject of this book. The concept made more sense than anything else I had read on the subject matter. What I loved about it is that even the daily practice of the principle was in itself wonderfully sublime—and enabled me to elevate my spirit to a state of indescribable bliss. And if that was all I got out of the practice, it would have been good enough for me. But what I didn't know then was that I was about to have the most transformative and exhilarating experience of my life.

As I continued to practice the greatest manifestation principle—which no one else was teaching at the time—my life began to change its trajectory quite rapidly. The turning point began on the 4th of July in 2008. I had spent that holiday weekend with my sister Beth's family in northern California. After the holiday picnic and fireworks were done, Beth asked me to join her in her home office because she had something to show me. She then confessed to me that she was about to lose her house to foreclosure because she and her husband, John—both real estate agents with practically no income in 2008—have been unable to pay their mortgage in several months. She pointed to a stack of bills on her desk, 7 inches thick, and said those were the bills they had been unable to pay. The only bills they were paying monthly were utility bills—and that was only because they needed to keep the lights on and water running in order to live. The family members who lived in Beth and John's house included an adult son, an adult daughter, and son-in-law—all of whom had lost their jobs that year—and 3 grandchildren. Beth and John could hardly get enough money to put food on the table for the eight members of their household.

There in her home office, my sister and I cried over the dire financial straits her family was in. Shortly thereafter, we were joined by John, who added that by Christmas that year, their family would be homeless and would have no place to live. They wouldn't even qualify to rent since they had bad credit, had filed for bankruptcy that year, and had no income to show to a prospective landlord. The three of us cried together till the wee hours of the morning.

When I returned home to Los Angeles after that holiday weekend, I began practicing the greatest manifestation principle which I had learned months earlier, with the intention of finding a way to get my sister and her family out of their seemingly hopeless predicament. I was mindful of the principle's doctrine that *any endeavor that is nourished and motivated by love* cannot help but succeed. But even as I practiced the principle, I had serious doubts as to how I—or anyone—could save Beth's family from losing their house and becoming destitute, homeless and hungry.

But despite my doubts, I persisted with the practice of the principle. Within a few days, I experienced an epiphany of sorts, which prompted me to write a book about a natural healing therapy that I had heard about in January 2008. I don't know how that idea just spontaneously popped into my head, but there it was. I guess I had hoped that writing the book and marketing it online could potentially generate enough money to at least feed my sister's family. The prospect of making enough money to save their house from foreclosure seemed an impossible task to me at that point, so I dared not desire that.

While practicing the principle, my unspoken prayer was that this humble business venture would produce a modest profit of $1,000 a month, which would be enough to at least feed my sister's household and maybe even pay for a portion of their utilities.

Within 5 weeks of the book idea first dawning on me, I had finished writing a 113-page book, which I titled *"The One-Minute Cure: The Secret to Healing Virtually All Diseases."* I wrote it under my pen name

Madison Cavanaugh.

The e-book was available for sale online by mid-August. When the e-book generated modest profits of $600 that first month, I was pleasantly surprised. I gave all of it to Beth, who gratefully used the money to feed her family.

What happened in the next few months can only be described as spectacularly miraculous: The profits I generated from the e-book (and later, the printed edition of the book) skyrocketed from $2,100 in September, to $13,000 in October, and $246,000 in April 2009. That same month, the book became the No. 1 Amazon bestseller in the Health, Body and Mind category for the first of 15 times, and it hit the milestone of generating cumulative sales of $1 million by July 2009.

The best part of all this was that I was able to share the profits with Beth, and this enabled her not just to resume paying her monthly mortgage but also pay all her monthly bills and support her family's needs once again. I still remember that November day when the book's profits enabled her to pay her monthly mortgage for the first time in almost a year. Her tears were unstoppable, and we both were elated beyond measure.

At that point, I was tempted to believe that all this was just a stroke of good fortune which *coincidentally* occurred after I began practicing the greatest manifestation principle—a one-time windfall that wouldn't last, or never come again. But I found the contrary to be true because that was just the beginning of the string of fortuitous events to come.

For instance, I finally had the financial means to do much-needed repairs on the roof of my mom's house. This spared my mom's life (and the lives of my sister Carla's family of five, who also lived in that house) when the biggest tropical storm made landfall two weeks after the roof was fixed. An engineer had told my mom that the roof would have come crashing down on all the occupants of the house—and most likely killed them— had I not come up with the money to get repairs done in time. I considered that a true *miracle*, if there ever was one.

With the financial blessings, which seemed to be gushing forth like a never-ending spring, I was also able to financially support many members of my family who had lost their jobs when the U.S. economy took a nosedive in 2008.

As of the time of this writing, *The One-Minute Cure* has generated **more than $7 million in revenue**! The astonishing profits from the book, which were above and beyond anything I could have imagined, enabled me to purchase my very first house in 2010—a mid-century modern **house in prestigious Beverly Hills, California**, and enabled me to pay off the mortgage in full soon thereafter.

The profits from *The One-Minute Cure* book also provided me with sufficient seed money to establish another company in 2010, which marketed anti-aging skincare products, as well as a third company selling organic nutritional supplements. Between 2010 through 2015, **each one of the 3 companies I owned was generating millions of dollars in revenue**.

A year after I merged the anti-aging skincare company with the nutritional supplement company, I was able to sell the company in February 2016 for a **substantial sum of $6,200,000**!

The financial good fortune that came into my life in a rapid-fire manner as a result of my consistent practice of the greatest manifestation principle was quite extraordinary, but it comprised only a small subset of the abundance that has made its way into *every aspect of my life*.

All the fortunate events and blessings that have come into my life are so numerous that they could fill an entire book. But suffice it to say that my life has been overflowing with miraculous things, such as healings, broken relationships mended, a deep spiritual connection with

God, and more love, joy and peace than I ever thought I deserved. So much so that at the present moment, I wake up every morning so thankful that I'm literally living a dream come true — the very best life I could ever have!

In the first edition of this book, I wrote the following words about what one should expect when practicing the greatest manifestation principle: *"The outcome you get may be different from what you had in mind, but it will be infinitely better than that which you desired."*

Those words weren't only absolutely true, but they were also prophetic in the context of my life. One only has to look at what has happened to me in the past 13 years, to know that what I got was infinitely better than what I desired! What I got was the very definition of *my best life*.

This is the reason I decided to change the sub-title of this second edition to: *How Quantum Physics and Spirituality Can Enable You to Manifest Your Best Life.* Manifesting one or two of your heart's desires—such as achieving a remarkable income, having a lucrative business, landing your ideal job, finding your soul mate, achieving your ideal weight—is only part of the equation. Oftentimes, once you accomplish one of your desires, you might find it doesn't fulfill you and you begin to feel it wasn't what you truly wanted after all.

Having your best life, on the other hand, means getting

all the good things you want—*in perfect balance*—which results in a life filled with good fortune, joy, peace, health and well-being, self-realization, an intimate connection to the divine, and a feeling of being complete, lacking nothing.

This is what I want for you, and is the reason I wrote the second edition of this book. If the story of how I achieved my best life serves as an inspiration to you, then I feel gratified because I know that your practice of the greatest manifestation principle will lead you to co-create your best life, too. Not just what most people regard as one's "best life"—but rather, what *you* regard as *your* best life.

I've added a new section in this edition, titled *How to Eliminate the Biggest Obstacles That Prevent You from Manifesting Your Heart's Desires,* which answers the question most people ask with regards to manifestation: **Why do some people manifest their heart's desires—but most don't?** It provides concrete methodology for removing the blocks that have been keeping you from successful manifesting, and reveals a profound concept which, when mastered, will provide you with the rarefied perspective of instantly having everything you desire—even before you manifest it into your life!

You may not realize it, but the moment you started reading this book, you already began the process of manifesting your best life. It's already present in your auric field—your energetic matrix—and all you have to do is stay the course. **That which you want to manifest is already within you—and it's already connected to the field of all possibilities, all potentialities.** The only thing keeping you from manifesting is the presence of a lower level of consciousness that is diametrically opposed to the greatest manifestation principle—and this sabotages your efforts to manifest your desires into reality.

If you are ready to learn the greatest manifestation principle, you will also discover the quickest way to let go of the lower level of consciousness that has kept you from manifesting your best life. The philosopher, Lao Tzu, wrote in the *Tao Te Ching*, "When the student is ready the teacher will appear." Because you are ready and in a state of receptiveness, you will promptly recognize the profound truth when it enters your field of awareness.

I am deeply overwhelmed by the enormity of the privilege of sharing this manifestation principle with you because I've seen its stunning outcomes in my life—and I know it's within your reach once you embrace and internalize the profound principle presented in this book.

Here's wishing you a life wherein miracles are an everyday occurrence.

— Carnelian Sage

Chapter 1

The Field of Infinite Potentiality

Imagine how your life would be if you could manifest all your desires into existence. What if all you had to do was wish for a loving relationship, an ideal job, perfect health, your dream house, a luxurious vacation, a brand new car–or anything you want–and it magically materialized in your life?

This is the overarching promise claimed by manifestation practitioners.

But just like the medieval science of alchemy—with its promise of turning base metals into gold—and other mystical enigmas like the philosopher's stone and the fountain of youth, manifestation always seems like an elusive dream—one that is beyond the grasp of average human beings.

One of the first books that ignited mainstream interest in the practice of manifestation was *Think and Grow Rich*, written in 1937 by Napoleon Hill. That book is the most widely acclaimed, influential book on personal success ever published, and is still in print to this day. Just as its title suggests, the book introduced the premise that riches begin with a state of mind, with definiteness of purpose, and can be achieved *with little or no hard work*. This concept of effortless creation has always been something that the world found irresistible.

About 70 years later, at the dawn of the twenty-first century, the Law of Attraction movement began to emerge, and this captured the imagination of the masses even more. The Law of Attraction is governed by the principle that **like attracts like**. Simply stated, it supports the premise that you attract to your life anything you give your energy, focus and attention to—whether wanted or unwanted. What you think about is what you create; what you give out is what you get back.

Everything in the universe—including our thoughts—are made of energy, which vibrates at specific frequencies. Different kinds of thoughts generate different kinds of vibrations, and vibrations of thought can actually be photographed. Positive thoughts have a high vibrational frequency, which means the waves move at a higher and faster rate. According to the precepts of the Law of Attraction, positive thoughts attract everything in the universe that is a vibrational match to one's thoughts—and that means everything from a dream house to a diamond necklace, a luxury car, an ideal job or a romantic relationship. Negative thoughts, on the other hand, have a low vibrational frequency, which means the waves move at a lower and slower rate. Therefore, they attract everything in the universe that's a vibrational match to those thoughts—and that means everything from a stopped-up sink in your house to getting into a car accident, getting fired from a job, getting sick, and so on.

The Law of Attraction is not a physical law like the law of gravity, the laws of motion, thermodynamics and the like. Rather, it's an **observation** of t*he tendency of things to materialize when they are held in one's mind.* There has been an *attempt* to link the Law of Attraction to science by way of its association with a tuning fork. If you hold a tuning fork in one hand and hit its tines against the heel of your other hand (i.e., "ding" it), it creates vibrations that move through the air. If you let the tines touch the surface of water, you see ripples, which is the visual evidence of vibration waves. If you ding the tuning fork in a room filled with different kinds of tuning forks calibrated to various pitches, you'll discover that only the tuning forks calibrated to the same frequency as the one you just dinged will vibrate, too. It's easy for many to conclude that objects with the same vibrational frequencies attract each other; therefore, high-vibration feelings and emotions will attract similarly high-vibration outcomes into one's life, won't they?

Not quite. Although the tuning fork certainly makes a stunning and graphic example, it's nothing more than a nice *metaphor*, which does <u>not</u> represent the true mechanism of how manifestation really works. But it's a convincing metaphor nonetheless.

The Law of Attraction principles that are currently being taught—such as *visualization of desire* and *gratitude for what one has*—are useful and important. If all that these principles accomplish is to get people to focus on positive things and things that make them feel good; allow them to dream of the things they want (instead of focus on what they don't want); eliminate their "why do bad things always happen to me" victim attitude; and inspire them to take charge of their thoughts and their destiny; it has provided a beneficial service indeed.

However, practicing the principles of the Law of Attraction with the expectation that it will manifest one's dream car, an ideal relationship, a beautiful house, abundant wealth, perfect health and all the good things in life, is an exercise in delusion. It's adopting the mistaken notion that the universe is like a cosmic restaurant that takes your orders (desires) and delivers them to you just as surely as a waiter takes your orders and delivers food to your table.

We all dream of working that kind of magic, but unfortunately, that's not how the principle behind true manifestation works. It is not the result of magic, but rather a weaving of quantum physics and spirituality into a field of possibilities from which you can consciously create your best life.

If you'd like to discover **the missing secret** and the *real power* behind manifestation, which will enable you to truly manifest your heart's desires, you'll find the answer in this book.

To provide you with a foretaste of the information you're about to discover, I present you with this foundation of true manifestation:

There is an infinite field of energy that surrounds and permeates all things, embodying all existence, both seen and unseen. Some call this energy field Source Energy, the quantum field, divine intelligence, the universal mind, the field of all possibilities, the Divine Creative Consciousness of Love—or its ultimate name, God. This field is without beginning or end, goes beyond time and space, and consists of pure boundless, immeasurable power and energy, vibrating higher and faster than the ordinary levels of human intellect and awareness can observe, comprehend or explain.

In this formless vibratory spiritual field of Infinite Potentiality lie all the hopes and dreams of all mankind— where all your desires are already an unformed potentiality waiting to manifest into existence. All human beings exist within this field, are part of it, and are connected to it—but most of us have lost our natural connection to it because of the emergence of the *ego*. The ego is your false self, an illusory idea that you construct in your consciousness about who and what you are. It is your ego that keeps you separate from this field, and makes you unable to access the field's power to bring you what you desire.

You can take anything you desire from formless to concrete expression simply by reconnecting with this field. The attainment of your desires, then, comes from not allowing your ego to think that it can *cause* things to happen or attract things to you by simply focusing on positive thoughts and feelings. It is when you transcend your ego, let go of your desires, and stay in harmony with this field, that your desires *can* and MUST necessarily manifest into existence.

The greatest manifestation principle in the world that is revealed in this book will enable you to realign yourself and stay in harmony with this field where all things are possible.

I invite you to read this book repeatedly and often. Simply reading a chapter, a page or even a paragraph from this book everyday will have a transformational effect—it will make you a different person and will have a profound impact on your energy level and personal growth. As you read and reflect on the material contained herein, layers of wisdom and insights will unfold that will accelerate your ability to effortlessly attract the things you really want. When you allow the power of the greatest manifestation principle in the world to permeate your awareness, tremendous results will begin to manifest in every area of your life.

The objective of this book is to correct any inaccuracies, dispel myths surrounding the process of manifestation—and more importantly, shed light on the most powerful manifestation principle in the world that no one is talking about. When you use this powerful manifestation principle while being connected to the quantum field—you enter the realm of miracles where the manifestation of all desires is truly possible.

This book is purposely brief because the greatest manifestation principle in the world is quite simple, as all great truths are. Although I refer to it as the "missing secret," it has actually never been a secret at all. It is a *spiritual truth* that has been used by ancient mystics to modern-day spiritual seekers, to people of all faiths—and everyone in between—with great success. But no one has ever discovered how to use that spiritual truth *in conjunction with* their manifestation practice to make the materialization of desires a *certainty*, instead of something merely *hoped for*. May the spiritual truth and the expansive way of seeing things that you will discover in this book, enable you to not only manifest your desires but allow you to find unbounded joy, love and peace in your life's journey.

The case histories I have studied of people that managed to succeed in manifesting their desires, invariably had this manifestation principle in place—but weren't aware that it was this manifestation principle that materialized their desires. A well-known motivational speaker who has achieved great success and abundant wealth, unconsciously uses this principle. Although his teachings encompass various techniques involving quantum physics, spiritual truths and the Law of Attraction, it was this *one* principle in particular that allowed all good things to continually show up in his life.

This is the reason why some people are astonishingly successful in manifesting desires—but most are not successful at all. Somewhere along the way, those who are successful somehow employ the greatest manifestation principle *without knowing it*—and that principle supplies the missing ingredient that completes the recipe for manifestation.

And *voila*! Their desires are manifested—and they're justifiably elated. However, since they are unaware of the real reason why their desire manifested, they erroneously assume it was because they focused on what they wanted; took their focus away from the things they didn't want; visualized their desire until it was so real they could almost touch it; and expressed gratitude every step of the way. Sadly, although this popular ask-believe-receive "formula" for manifesting desires *seems* to make sense—and is even supported by scripture—it is <u>not</u> what causes desires to manifest.

That's why oftentimes, when people who were successful at manifesting one desire try to duplicate their success using the "formula" they implemented before, they fail to produce the same successful results—and their desire does not manifest the second time around and beyond. That's also why the process of manifestation has never produced any degree of consistency or certainty in getting results.

The practice of manifestation, as based on the teachings of the books and courses released in the last 100 years, employs a *hit-or-miss methodology* that has been passed down through the years. Some practitioners report positive results (most of which have nothing to do with true manifestation), but the majority experience little or no results. Most of the failures are never reported, which explains why most people are unaware of the dismal success rate (or conversely, the disheartening failure rate) of those who try their hand at practicing manifestation.

Therein lies the partial truth in practically every concept known to man. People take their limited understanding of something, and represent it to others as *the* truth. The people who are exposed to the distorted information, in turn, represent it to others as *the* truth. Ultimately, all we really have is fractured versions of the truth—all of us knowing a small part but never the whole. And you know what they say about people knowing just enough to be dangerous!

How I Found the Greatest Manifestation Principle

The concept of manifesting desires has been a great interest of mine since 1981. I've studied the principles of quantum physics, and searched for that secret alchemy that would turn thoughts into things. Its promise was too irresistible and intriguing to ignore. It seemed like the next best thing to having a magic wand that you can wave, and cause your wishes to come true.

Little did I know that I wasn't destined to discover the real secret to successful manifesting until 26 years later.

For 26 years, I researched and investigated all known avenues of manifestation, including quantum mechanics, paranormal studies, esoteric sciences, affirmation techniques, hypnosis, visualization, scriptural secrets, and everything else in between. And yet all that knowledge had gotten me no closer to manifesting my desires into existence. Apart from small victories and experiencing a sprinkling of minor pleasant occurrences (that might have been the result of confirmation bias or the *experimenter effect* discussed in Chapter 3), I had yet to find evidence that one could truly alchemize one's thoughts into physical existence.

It was rather peculiar that back in 1997 when I vigilantly practiced everything I knew about manifestation, I suffered the most severe financial setback in my life and I came dangerously close to bankruptcy. I would have declared bankruptcy had it not been for the financial help of a loved one who bailed me out temporarily. That ensuing financial slump and career meltdown lasted for four years even as I continued to practice manifestation the way I knew it back then. I couldn't understand why this was happening—and why I wasn't attracting the prosperity I desired.

In 2004, I underwent an ultrasound scan, and several tumors were found in my body. Once again, I used the standard manifestation principles—combined with healthy eating habits—to make them disappear, and avert the need for the major surgery that my doctor urged me to have. I had also read about the healing power of laughter in Dr. Norman Cousins's book, *Anatomy of an Illness as Perceived by the Patient*—so I watched funny TV shows and movies whenever I could—all to no avail. I immersed myself in positive thoughts and practiced a healthy lifestyle, but one of the tumors grew to the size of a small grapefruit within a matter of weeks!

I couldn't believe this was happening to me!

As a result of the tumors, I became so weak and dangerously anemic that I was rushed to the Emergency Room at a nearby hospital on two occasions, and had to endure two separate inpatient stays within two weeks of each other. I finally had to agree to undergo major surgery to remove the tumors, all of which were, thankfully, benign.

That setback was probably the pivotal point in my adventures (and misadventures) with the practice of manifestation. I began to ponder the reasons why I was not getting the results I desired. For that matter, I took a long, hard look at the reasons why all the people I've known, who were using the same standard manifestation principles that I was, were still struggling financially and weren't getting as much out of life as they pretended they were getting.

I began to wonder whether the practice of manifestation was just a hoax after all.

A colleague of mine named Brad, who practiced the Law of Attraction faithfully not only did not achieve the successful business enterprise that he visualized every day, but instead found himself in a long string of disastrous events that led to a debt of over $200,000.

A friend of mine, an aspiring actress named Emma,

practiced the Law of Attraction for a year to get a better job so that she wouldn't have to wait on tables at a restaurant. She's still stuck in that job to this day. To make matters worse, the restaurant cut back her hours, which left her struggling financially to make ends meet. Try as she might, she couldn't seem to find another job. Her real desire was to break into the acting field. She had been visualizing herself as a successful working actress, but none of her positive thoughts have landed her a single role, even after endless auditions.

A female singer-songwriter acquaintance of mine named Ainsley had always dreamed of winning a Grammy award for her music. She's been visualizing herself accepting a Grammy Award—and her vision was so vivid that she even had her acceptance speech all written out. She had been using the Law of Attraction for years, but she has yet to see any evidence that her dream will ever happen.

I can give hundreds of examples of failed attempts to manifest desires by people who have used the Law of Attraction, or standard manifestation practices for a few months to several years. And it's not for lack of trying since countless people have faithfully followed these principles for decades, and are still left wondering why they are not yet rich, are not yet restored to health, still don't have the dream house, dream car, dream job or dream relationship they've been focusing on for a long time.

And then by accident, I discovered the missing secret that turned my life around—and the lives of everyone with whom I shared the secret. Here's how it happened:

In 2007, I attended a lecture given by an individual whom I consider to be one of the most deeply spiritual individuals I have ever encountered. The lecture was not about manifestation but rather about spiritual truths that can be applied to our everyday lives. One of the truths he revealed struck a chord in me. It was so profound in its simplicity, and yet wielded more power than anything I could imagine.

I began to wonder whether it was the secret to manifesting one's desires.

I didn't have to wonder long because shortly after I started infusing that spiritual truth in my practice of manifestation, my life was literally transformed overnight. I was divinely prompted—and enabled, against all odds— to write and publish a book in 5 weeks' time titled, *The One-Minute Cure: The Secret to Healing Virtually All Diseases*. As explained in the Introduction, this book amassed a 7-figure fortune for me. But more than the financial wealth that the book brought me, the most gratifying thing was receiving reports from countless people all over the world who, after reading the book, were healed of diseases they were suffering from—some of which were life-threatening, "incurable" or terminal—and restored to perfect health. That was an immensely heartwarming feeling that money could not buy.

On top of the financial wealth I amassed, stubborn health problems disappeared, broken relationships were repaired, and I experienced love, joy, peace and a sense of fulfillment greater than I ever thought possible. To this day, I wake up every day to a life that exceeds the "best life" that I once desired for myself.

It was the incredible series of fortuitous circumstances that descended upon my life over the last 13 years that prompted me to write this second edition of this book. I want to shout it from the rooftops so that more readers all over the world can experience something similar to what I've experienced, by practicing the greatest manifestation principle in the world.

Upon examining the successes of people who have managed to get significant results from the standard practice of manifestation or the Law of Attraction, I observed that this spiritual truth was also an essential factor in the manifestation of their desires. Usually, they didn't even realize that they were exercising the power of that spiritual truth, and weren't even aware it had anything to do with the materialization of their desires.

Individuals of great accomplishment throughout human history have also invariably aligned themselves with this spiritual truth. Whenever they attributed the source of their power to something greater than themselves, more often than not, it was this manifestation principle that was at the heart of their success. The same is true of individuals who have been miraculously healed of lingering—and even terminal—illnesses.

I remember the first time I realized the profound effect of this manifestation principle. I was overwhelmed by the phenomenal implications that it would have on people's lives and the world. Tears of joy came pouring out of my eyes out of gratitude for the gift of spiritual discernment, and the realization of this truth.

I have named this spiritual truth *the greatest manifestation principle in the world*. Because of the staggering transformation the practice of this principle has had on my life, and in the lives of those who have practiced it in their own lives, it has removed all doubt in my mind that it works without fail. The mechanism by which it works is explained by both quantum physics and spirituality, which lies in the nonlinear realm. I invite you to test the principle and prove to yourself that it certainly works in ways that go far beyond your expectations.

Chapter 2

The Science Behind Manifestation

The process of manifestation is a weaving together of quantum physics and spirituality. Most people are intimidated—or even scared off—by the term "quantum physics". Rest assured that you will not need to learn this complex and "mysterious" science. My objective for including an overview of quantum physics in this book is to present real scientific evidence that manifestation is a discipline that truly yields one's desired outcomes. More importantly, I aim to dispel the belief among skeptics that manifestation is just an insubstantial "airy-fairy" approach or a pseudo-scientific way of turning desires into reality.

The discussion of quantum physics in the following pages will be intentionally brief, and will delve only into the aspects of quantum physics that are directly involved with the practice of manifestation.

What is Quantum Physics and How Does It Differ from Classical Physics?

Classical physics (also called *Newtonian physics*) is a branch of science that explains mechanical events—those that involve matter affecting matter through *force*—using the laws of motion and gravitation. It was formulated in the late seventeenth century by English physicist Sir Isaac Newton (1642-1727). Newtonian physics is the study of things that are *manifest*—that is, the visible, tangible parts of the world that we can measure and perceive with our five senses. Our perception of reality is normally from the standpoint of Newtonian physics.

Quantum physics, on the other hand, is a branch of science that studies the physical phenomena and behavior of microscopic, atomic and sub-atomic particles. It specifies the laws of motion that the microscopic objects obey. It explains events that involve **energy influencing matter**. Quantum physics is completely different from the classical physics that we learned in school. This science has revealed a whole new aspect of reality, one that is not necessarily observable with the five senses.

Quantum physics explores the relationship of energy and matter. Understanding it confounds most people because it contradicts our common sense—i.e., our Newtonian view of the world—yet it is the most comprehensive theory in all of science.

From Wave to Particle — Unmanifest to Manifest

One of the theories that emerged from the study of quantum physics is that we human beings influence the fabric of life. The sub-atomic particles, or *quanta* (Latin: plural for quantum) are particles that do not exist at a specific point in space and time—unlike physical things like a chair, a house or a car—but also behave like waves—*waves of probability (or potentiality)* that <u>could</u> exist at various points in space and time. The moment we observe these waves, they turn into a "physical" *particle* that now exists at a specific point in space and time.

But here's the part that seems supernatural: Once we withdraw our attention from that particle, that particle "collapses" and becomes a *wave of potentiality* again. This, in itself, is an exciting prospect because moment by moment, a new reality is created. It's an amazing dance in which the whole universe is constantly being recreated. It seems like the stuff of science fiction, but this fascinating way sub-atomic units behave is a **scientific fact** that is observable in the laboratory.

The study of quantum physics has verified that **a thing can only exist if it is observed**. This is referred to as the *observer effect*, which pertains to the disturbance of an observed system by the act of observation. The sub-atomic particles organize themselves according to the influence of the mind of the observer. When something is observed with a specific *intention,* the sub-atomic particles organize themselves into atoms, and then molecules, until they materialize into something in the physical world that is visible, tangible and measurable. In other words, the waves become particles that eventually turn into what humans experience as physical existence.

The most fascinating quantum physics research—which lends credence to the superpower inherent in every human being (called conscious co-creation)—involves the double-slit experiment. *Every single thought is energy, and it instantly and directly influences the quantum field of all possibilities.* The double-slit experiment demonstrates a phenomenon that defies logic, as follows: Sub-atomic particles of matter have wave characteristics, and the very act of observing a particle has a dramatic effect on its *behavior*.

To summarize, our universe, emotions and our thoughts are made of energy. Every human being has the capacity to influence the creation of matter (from waves of potentiality to particles) and affect one's environment through the power of one's *observation* and *intention*. An observer then, is able to influence the *behavior* of particles—but the question is: How does one influence particles in a way that materializes one's desires? This has always been the eternal mystery.

One could conceivably infuse the particles with any random intention, thoughts and emotions, but in doing so, the behavior of the particles would behave in an erratic and unpredictable fashion—and one is not likely to get what one intended or desired. This is the reason why the process of manifestation has largely been a hit-or-miss proposition for most people.

However, if one were to infuse particles—and the energy field—with the greatest manifestation principle (revealed in Chapter 3), it exponentially increases the likelihood that the sub-atomic particles will organize themselves into atoms, and then molecules, until they materialize into that object, event or set of circumstances that one had intended or desired.

Why? Because the greatest manifestation principle is **the most powerful creative force in the universe**.

Suffice it to say that every human being has the capacity to influence the creation of matter through the power of one's observation, intention <u>and</u>—most importantly—the greatest manifestation principle. You then can become a conscious co-creator since you operate in conjunction with the quantum field to create objects, experiences or the life you desire.

The operative term here is "conscious co-creation". Most people rarely do conscious co-creation—perhaps largely because they aren't aware they could do such a thing. So they *unconsciously* create their experience of life by default. More importantly, most people who attempt manifestation—such as the millions who have tried practicing the Law of Attraction—aren't aware that in addition to consciously co-creating with the energy field, there is also a principle that needs to be present in order to produce the outcome they desire.

One can think of conscious co-creation as one would a 3D printer that can print a wide variety of things—such as vehicles, tools, clothes, toys, musical instruments, medical supplies, houses, and even human organs and body parts. To 3D print any object, you first create a *blueprint* of the object you want to "print". Once you have a finished design and the materials (such as plastic, metal, powders, resins, carbon fiber, paper, graphite) are assembled, you now have the *components* to create. But nothing is created until you press the button on the 3D printer, which begins the process. The 3D printer takes your blueprint and starts pulling the material it needs from the supply of materials—and adds one layer of the object at a time onto the plate until you have a fully formed structure.

Likewise, when you embark on the endeavor of conscious co-creation, you start with the design in your mind—that is, your desire of how you want your life to be (blueprint). All the raw materials you need (components) to create what you desire are already available in the energy field as waves of potentiality. At this point you have everything you need to create—but nothing happens until you put the greatest manifestation principle (3D printer) into action. The principle, which is the most powerful creative force in the universe, takes your design and starts pulling the material it needs from the vast supply of waves of potentiality (the energy field) and begins to turn the waves into sub-atomic particles, which turn into atoms, and then molecules—taking unformed potentiality into physical existence—particle-by-particle until you have the fully formed objects, circumstances, experiences—and the best life—you desire.

The important thing to remember is this: If you don't fuel your practice of manifestation or conscious co-creation with the greatest manifestation principle, you're bound to experience hit-or-miss results as a consequence of your unconscious thinking. You may even unconsciously create the things you don't want in your life.

This conscious co-creation is the very basis of manifestation, deliberate creation and the materialization of desires. But the formula is only complete when you combine it with the power of the greatest manifestation principle (see Chapter 3).

As defined above, classical (Newtonian) physics is a world that necessitates the use of **force** to accomplish desired outcomes; while quantum physics (which focuses on the workings of energy) is a world that employs intrinsic **power** to accomplish the same. The latter lends itself to *effortless co-creation*. In the section below titled, *Elevate Your Emotional State: The Easy Way and the Hard Way*, is a road-map for elevating your consciousness to a level that employs power instead of force to rapidly manifest one's desires.

Our commonsense assumptions—and our Newtonian conditioning—impose limitations on what we believe is possible. In the strange universe of quantum physics, where particles can be in two places at once ... ... where two objects—even though separated in space— are still connected ... and where objects can disappear and reappear in a new place without having traveled to get there ... we now know why it's possible to manifest into existence things that defy logic, and which we once thought impossible or unattainable.

Elevate Your Emotional State: The Easy Way and the Hard Way

It is a well-known fact that our emotions consist of energy that produce vibrational frequencies, which in turn, affect our bodies at the cellular level. But how do we measure the frequencies of various emotions—and what do those frequencies mean in the context of manifestation?

Sir David R. Hawkins, MD, PhD, an internationally renowned spiritual teacher, psychiatrist, physician, and researcher, developed the Map of Consciousness® which he introduced in his book, *Power versus Force.* Dr. Hawkins calibrated human consciousness into 17 emotional stages based on their vibrational frequencies, which were measured via kinesiology (muscle monitoring or muscle testing). He divided the levels of consciousness (expressed in emotional states) into 17 different frequencies, measured in Hertz units. 1 Hertz (Hz) corresponds to 1 vibration per second, 60 Hz corresponds to 60 vibrations per second. He named this the Map of Consciousness®.

Emotional Frequency Chart

Energetic Frequency	Level
700-1000Hz	Enlightenment
600Hz	Peace
540Hz	Joy
500Hz	Love
400Hz	Reason
350Hz	Acceptance
310Hz	Willingness
250Hz	Neutrality
200Hz	Courage
175Hz	Pride
150Hz	Anger
125Hz	Desire
100Hz	Fear
75Hz	Grief
50Hz	Apathy
30Hz	Guilt
1-20Hz	Shame

Strong — Weak

Creative Energy — Destructive Energy

In Hawkins's Map, the lower the vibrational frequency, the more *negative or destructive* the energy is. The emotions of shame, guilt, apathy, grief, fear, desire, anger, and pride all vibrate to the frequencies ranging from 1 Hz to 175 Hz. These are regarded as the lower levels of consciousness, the destructive emotional states, wherein one needs to use *force* to accomplish or create anything. On the other end of the spectrum, courage, neutrality, willingness, acceptance, reason, love, joy, peace, and enlightenment comprise the higher levels of consciousness and emotional states, with frequencies measuring between 200 Hz to 1000 Hz. These are regarded as the higher levels of consciousness, the *creative* emotional states, wherein one employs *power*, not force, to accomplish or create anything.

Which emotional states do you think would be the ideal states in which to manifest your desires?

It goes without saying that the emotional states corresponding to the higher levels of consciousness are more conducive to manifestation. The higher the better. That's because at those levels, you're operating with power, which means you can engage in *effortless creation* versus operating at the lower levels of consciousness wherein you're having to struggle or *exercise force* to accomplish your desires.

However, achieving those higher emotional states is easier said than done since most human beings often live their daily lives immersed in emotions at the lower (destructive) spectrum of the Map. One is usually unable to climb the ladder of emotions to reach an emotional state corresponding to the higher levels of consciousness. Why? Because negative emotions are some of the most challenging things to overcome and rise above—especially emotions associated with shame, guilt and fear. Most human beings operate at those lower levels of consciousness all day long, and oftentimes, even when they're asleep.

Fortunately, there's an easy solution to this dilemma.

1) It's helpful to have the Emotional Frequency Chart on hand in order to identify the emotional state you're in at any given moment, and determine whether you're in a destructive or creative level of consciousness. You can use this emotional guidance system for greater alignment with your highest good. A simple shift in frequency can change depression to peace, anger to stillness, and fear to enthusiasm. Learning to manage your own energy state can put you on track with your destiny—the life you're built for. You have a choice about the way you feel and what your life can be.

2) Once you've identified your current emotional state, you can do the spiritual exercise described in Chapter 4, which will enable you to effectively bypass the lower levels of consciousness and go

straight to the level of Love, where your body will be vibrating at 500 Hz or above within a few minutes.

By doing the aforementioned spiritual exercise, you can easily let go of the low-vibration emotional states (hate, guilt, fear, shame, avarice) so that you can experience the higher levels.

You're able to free yourself from negative or low vibrations instantly, feel a sense of euphoria as though you already have what you want to manifest in your life even before it actually manifests into existence.

How Heart-Centered Emotions Can Alter DNA

DNA is a nucleic acid that carries the genetic information in the cell. It is known as the "blueprint" of life because it governs the development and functions of humans and all living organisms.

It's a widely held belief that DNA, which is shaped like a double helix, has a fixed structure and cannot be changed. But a recent study from the Institute of HeartMath has shed startling results that challenge what we thought we knew about DNA.

In the study, human DNA was placed in a sealed test tube. Test subjects trained to **generate focused feelings of deep love** were able to intentionally cause a change in the shape of the DNA.

Negative emotions produced at will, cause the two strands that comprise human DNA to wind more tightly. Heart-centered feelings of love and appreciation generated by the research subjects, caused the DNA strands to unwind and exhibit positive changes in just two minutes. When those feelings were absent, no changes in the DNA were observed.

This may be the first scientific evidence of the long-held theory that emotion greatly affects our health and quality of life, and is proof positive that we can communicate with our DNA through emotion—and thus, change the very blueprint of our health and our lives.

Determination vs. Attraction - Power vs. Force

Almost everyone who has accomplished anything knows that being focused or passionate about achieving a goal or a dream will lead one to move in the same direction as their predominant thoughts. For instance, people might envision themselves as having $100,000 in a savings account, and they consequently *take action* on that image—by juggling three jobs, budgeting their money, skipping vacations and unnecessary luxuries, etc.—eventually saving up the $100,000. That's <u>not</u> manifestation at work. That's simply **determination** to accomplish a goal. And it required great effort or **force** to make it happen.

Real manifestation, on the other hand, is a phenomenon that happens when people envision themselves as *having* a particular desired result—and ideal opportunities, people, resources, circumstances, events and situations that contribute to that desired result, manifest themselves *without any prompting*. It requires no force to make it happen, but relies instead on a **power** greater than themselves—the greatest manifestation principle being the most essential of them all. This doesn't mean that some action is not required—but that action is done in a natural, easy manner as a result of the principle of spontaneous right action.

The Principle of Spontaneous Right Action

Spontaneous right action means that when one reaches a high level of consciousness—such as the levels of consciousness corresponding to Love, Joy, Peace and Enlightenment on the Map of Consciousness®—all of one's thoughts and actions are fully in accord with all the laws of nature.

They are "right" actions because they are appropriate to the time and circumstances, and **support every intention** at every level of creation.

The actions are "spontaneous" because it is not necessary for the conscious mind to calculate and be aware of every possible influence it can have before choosing to act. One's actions may or may not follow logic, because the impulse for natural behavior springs from a level which is beyond logic. One simply acts in a natural, easy manner and the cosmic intelligence operating within unbounded awareness, automatically produces action that is in harmony with nature and one's own good.

"There is only one choice, out of the infinity of choices available in every second, that will create happiness for you as well as for those around you. And when you make that one choice, it will result in a form of behavior that is called *spontaneous right action*. Spontaneous right action is the right action at the right moment. It's the right response to every situation as it happens. It's the action that nourishes you and everyone else who is influenced by that action." — Deepak Chopra. *The Seven Spiritual Laws of Success*

The thing to remember is that holding your desired results in mind is just *one part* of the equation. Your actions, decisions and feelings figure significantly in what's manifested into your life. Collectively, your thoughts, spontaneous right actions, and the quality of your connection to the energy field contribute to an infinite number of possibilities.

As you begin the practice of manifesting your best life, resist the urge to ask the question: *"When is it going to happen?"* When you have such a reaction, it shows that you haven't arrived at the place of trust that your desires are already an eventuality waiting to happen. What you may not realize is that in questioning the status of the manifestation of your desires, you actually slow down the process of their fulfillment because you've allowed your ego to dictate a time-frame. This then means you're setting up *resistance*, instead of just *allowing* the universe (energy field) to bring your desires at the appropriate time.

Another common reaction that slows down manifestation is when you pre-determine *how* your desires will be manifested. Again, this reaction is generated by the ego wanting to control the outcome. If, for example, your desire is to manifest $10,000, your ego "figures out" how it wants you to have it, such as by getting a salary raise, landing a large business deal, winning the lottery, or any one of a number of ways. The problem is that your ego has severe limitations—it only knows what is in the scope of your experience or knowledge. It doesn't have access to the myriad possibilities that are beyond your imagination or your concept of what's "real" or "achievable". Therefore, you become attached to the outcome and you *look* for the evidence you expect to see, and may *overlook* the amazing opportunities that the universe delivers. Again, this is a form of resistance to the flow of the universe. It's like putting a huge boulder in the middle of a rushing river—and slowing down the speed by which the manifestation of your desires arrives at your banks.

Don't Resist the Flow

There's a story about a group of Chinese men walking through the woods beside a rushing river. Suddenly, they spotted the body of an old man bobbing up and down in the roaring rapids. Thinking the old man was dead, they ran to the river's edge trying to figure out how they were going to fish the body out of the water so that it wouldn't be swept out to sea. Their discussion came to an abrupt halt when the old man, who they had thought was dead, emerged out of the water, dried himself off and started walking away. The men ran after the old man and asked, "How did you survive in that water? No one could swim in that water without being killed." "It is really easy," the old man replied. "I just went up when the water went up, and down when the water went down."

It would require volumes to explain the ramifications of genetic predisposition, collective consciousness, karma and a host of other factors that play a role in bringing about events, circumstances, situations and conditions in life. One cannot fully discuss those subjects without being prepared to delve into controversial subjects such as why people are born into specific circumstances, geographic locations, and social strata. One must accept the fact that bad things cannot be simplistically explained as things that people attracted to themselves.

When bad things do happen, a person is likely to blame himself (or herself) for attracting the bad thing. Their mind perceives that the negative circumstances—such as getting into an accident, the death of a loved one, getting fired from their job, illness, or even small things like not finding an ideal parking space—are their fault, and they attracted those circumstances through the thoughts and feelings they've had in this lifetime. They then react with feelings of inadequacy, guilt, frustration, failure, fear or denial—and they project those internal emotions upon the world. In addition, they operate in the destructive emotional states, as defined by the Map of Consciousness®, which are not conducive to manifesting one's best life.

Suffice it to say, therefore, that *some* bad things do happen as a consequence of you vibrationally attracting such things to yourself through the negative thoughts and feelings you emit. The majority of bad things, however, are *karmically propelled*—that is, they are due to one or more of the unlimited combinations of thoughts, feelings, decisions, actions and other factors (not only *yours* but also those of *others*), contributing to the energy field, which in turn brings about events, circumstances, conditions and situations.

Much as we, as human beings, are inclined to put labels on all things, or impose our theories about what causes this or that, there is no exact science for figuring out exactly what combination of factors causes a particular thing to happen to a person, or a group of persons at a given time or place. Release yourself from self-blame when something bad happens to you. Don't fault yourself for it because more often than not, you had no *direct influence* on the outcome, any more than the victims of September 11 or Hurricane Katrina consciously (or unconsciously) attracted the disaster to themselves.

The best thing to do is to let go of all experiences that you perceive to be undesirable or unfortunate, and trust instead in the higher providential (karmic) order of things. Know that good things happen through the good thoughts, feelings, decisions and actions that you sow into the energy field. In Chapter 3, you will discover the single most powerful thing you can sow into that field that results in all good things.

Letting Go of Your Desires

One recurrent "rule" that many manifestation teachers always preach to their students is this: One must not focus on what one does <u>not</u> want (such as debt, grief, heartbreak, weight problems, financial problems, and other "normal" things that people unconsciously focus on)—but instead focus on what one *wants.*

While focusing on what you want is infinitely better than focusing on what you don't want, the absolute best way to get what you want in life is to *let go of wanting it in the first place.* This is probably the most important distinction between the current teachings on manifesting and the greatest manifestation principle. This point of departure is also probably the most difficult to accept and adopt because it *seems* to go against the principles of positive thinking, and the traditional procedure for manifesting desires.

However, when you fully understand and embrace the principle of letting go of desires, that's when you'll truly begin to manifest them consistently. When you're willing to surrender your desire to the divine, what you get is infinitely better than what you desired in the first place.

Here's how the process of desire works:

The moment you create a desire in your mind, you

create its opposite at that very instant. This is called the *positionality of duality*. In plain English, what this means is when you take a position about something—anything— such as "I intend to be rich," its polar opposite (in this case, poverty or lack of wealth), necessarily has to appear because of the inherent duality of all thought. You cannot perceive wealth except against the background of poverty (or the absence of wealth), nor can you perceive happiness except against the background of unhappiness. Every position that you take exists only relative to its opposite. In Chinese philosophy, this is called the *yin and yang* principle—the two opposing forces in the universe.

Consider this: How would you know something is noisy if you don't have its opposite—silence— against which to define it? Likewise, you can't perceive darkness except as the absence of light, and one can't envision wealth without simultaneously envisioning the absence of it. You can't really know joy unless you understand the concept of sadness or sorrow.

Furthermore, when you desire or want to have something in your life, say, a million dollars, it reinforces the reality that you don't have a million dollars. "Wanting" things reinforces a state of *lack* and keeps you in a state of *wanting*. Focusing on this brings you more lack.

Contrary to popular belief, it's <u>not</u> your mental focus that causes your desires to happen—but rather, it is **how**

well you connect to, or how much you are in harmony with the energy field, which is responsible for all of creation. Everything you are, including your emotions, feelings, beliefs and prayers in every moment, represents your ongoing communication with the energy field. And the circumstances in your life are the energy field's response to your communication.

That is why manifestation often *seems* to work in an erratic hit-or-miss fashion. It seems to work for some people, but not for others. It seems to work under certain conditions, and not in others. Actually, it works all the time—but not in the way you've been taught.

You already *know* at the deepest level of your being what you desire—there's no need to *focus* on it. You simply connect to the energy field, and *allow* your heart's desires to manifest. In some spiritual traditions, this is explained thus: *Those who seek God shall lack no good thing.*

This then is the essence of co-creation. Your ego may delude you into thinking that your thought vibrations are manifesting or creating your desired outcomes. The truth is that you never do the creating yourself. It's always a co-creation with God, with the universe, with the Source of All, with the energy field that quantum physicists call the quantum field.

All that's required of you is that you transcend your ego, and just allow the energy field to bring you what your heart desires. Let go of the state of "wanting" and be in the state of "having" or "accepting" instead. The energy field encompasses all things; therefore, it also encompasses everything that you find lacking in your life. When you fully embrace the truth that you are inextricably connected to this energy field, and that you're not a separate entity fending for yourself in the vast frontier of the cosmos, you will begin to realize that you're already connected with everything you want.

Instead of focusing on your desire, a better strategy would be to hold in mind that which you desire <u>without</u> adding desire to it. This means that you can picture yourself living in abundant wealth, for instance, but detach yourself from the state of wanting wealth. That way, there's no positionality—i.e., you're not taking a position. You're simply envisioning something that's already real in the energy field. One way of doing this is by affirming, "I *accept* that I have abundant wealth" or, in the case of a relationship, "I *accept* that I have a loving and blissful relationship."

The emotional state of *desire* ranks among the lowest levels of vibration (frequency of 125 Hz) in the Map of Consciousness® (see page 39). That means desire is among the *destructive* emotional states, wherein one needs to *struggle* or exercise *force* to accomplish or create anything. The vibrational frequency of desire is <u>not</u> the ideal springboard for manifesting your best life.

When you do accept what you desire, you must come from the elevated standpoint of being connected to the energy field. In this way, you allow your desire to transform itself from the unmanifest (formless potential) to the manifest. If you operate from the ego, however, your ego will come up with a host of objections to prove that what you're affirming is not true.

This may seem like mere semantics to you, but the truth remains that we live in a semantic universe and our reality is molded by language. The language we use in our everyday lives puts us in either empowering or disempowering states—sometimes without our knowing it—and whenever we can, we must choose language that empowers us.

Even the semantics, however, are eclipsed by the deep and profound spiritual truth about what truly causes everything we want to happen in our lives. This truth is not—nor has it ever been—a secret. It is something that has been available to all since the beginning of time— something held sacred and taught in all the major spiritual traditions, as well as all the spiritual books, including the Bible. The only thing that has been a secret is that people haven't known—until now—that this spiritual truth is the greatest manifestation principle in the world, and is the missing ingredient that makes the practice of manifesting powerful.

In fact, whenever the Law of Attraction has been shown to work, more often than not, it is this principle that caused it to work. And this principle is the subject of the next chapter.

Chapter 3

To Love is to Live

> "Love is the most powerful and still the most unknown energy of the world." – Pierre Teilhard de Chardin

Critics often deplore the materialistic ideals that the practice of standard manifestation or the Law of Attraction propagates. That's because most people who practice manifestation are drawn almost magnetically into the realm of materialism. They gravitate to self-centered acquisitions such as houses, cars, jewelry, vacations, etc.

One important thing to bear in mind is that it is <u>never</u> materialism or the desire for personal gain that manifests your desires. Therefore, for as long as your desires are motivated by materialism, personal gain or other selfish interests, you can visualize your desires all day long and yet you may never get what you want. One might argue that there are people and corporate entities that have acquired millions by operating from selfish and sometimes even downright ruthless and unscrupulous principles. Perhaps what one should consider are the multi-millions those people and companies *don't* make because they espouse selfish interests.

In practicing the Law of Attraction, while it's possible to observe good things happening in your life, more often than not, it is either *confirmation bias* or the *observer-expectancy effect* that may be causing you to observe those good things. Confirmation bias, in the context of psychology and cognitive science, is one's tendency to search for or interpret new information in a way that confirms one's preconceived beliefs—and ignore information and interpretations which contradict such preconceived beliefs.

The observer-expectancy effect (also called the *experimenter effect*) is a similar bias found in scientific research when a researcher expects a given result, and therefore unconsciously manipulates an experiment in order to find that result. To eliminate that effect in clinical studies, the double-blind methodology is often used.

In the standard practice of manifestation, you're directed to expect good things to happen to you as a result of positive, high-frequency thoughts. When you do this, your level of alertness is raised so that when events do occur (that may or may not have anything to do with the attraction principle), you not only *notice* them—you *magnify* them, and point to them as evidence that your manifestation practice works.

So if standard manifestation practices—or the Law of Attraction—don't work, what does? There is a powerful manifestation principle that dramatically increases the likelihood that your desires will materialize. Let me tell you about some studies that will illustrate this powerful principle.

Research has been conducted in recent years to shed some light on **spectacular athletic achievements**. What causes an athlete to excel in an athletic event, and even break through a performance barrier to a new level of human possibility? Proceeding from the proven axiom that the human body becomes stronger or weaker depending on one's mental state, researchers asked the test athletes to hold in mind either positive or negative *motives* for wanting to win the athletic event they were about to enter. They then measured the athletes' muscle strength using a clinical kinesiological muscle testing method that has been used as a diagnostic technique and verified widely over the past 35 years.

The researchers discovered that when the athlete held in mind selfish motives for winning, such as the hope of becoming a star, making a lot of money, or defeating an opponent, the muscle tested weak. But when the athlete held in mind noble motives such as the dedication of their performance to someone they *love*, the honor of their country or their sport, or the joy of exerting maximum effort for the sake of excellence, the muscle tested powerfully strong! It was concluded that when athletes are awash in the belief that their excellence goes beyond personal ambition and accomplishment, and that it's a gift to mankind as a demonstration of man's potential, their bodies go strong and remain strong throughout a competitive event, often transcending ordinary human limitations.

Research has also been done to shed some light on the **miracle of spontaneous recovery from illness**. What causes a person who is suffering from an incurable, and often lingering, disease or sickness to be healed spontaneously and restored to perfect health—usually without any medical intervention? It was discovered that frequently, there was a significant increase in the sick person's *capacity to love*, accompanied by the *awareness of the importance of love* as a healing factor.

Conversely, it has been observed that in those whose disease progressed rapidly, there was a marked increase in fear (which is the contrarian opposite of love), as well as anxiety, doubt, depression and stress.

A California woman named Sylvia, who had suffered from Stage 4 lymphoma, reported that prior to receiving her cancer diagnosis, she had felt *unloved* for a long time. She had feared her marriage was on the rocks and that her husband was not supportive of her; she endured tremendous discord with her in-laws; and her marriage eventually ended in a hostile divorce. Her oncologist, who is also the head of one of the most prestigious cancer centers in the country, a medical professional who normally deals only in hard science, had the wisdom to tell Sylvia about recognizing the importance of love in her healing. She ended every visit with Sylvia with the words, "I love you" – words that are seldom said by a doctor to a patient. Sylvia believes that her doctor was the catalyst that enabled her to allow love to become the central focus of her healing, and eventually, she was declared cancer-free. As of the time of this writing, Sylvia is still alive, 29 years after her late-stage cancer diagnosis.

Masaru Emoto, a creative and visionary Japanese researcher, observed that water reacts to different environmental conditions, music, and even pollution. This led him and his colleagues to conduct experiments to see how thoughts and words affect water. They used specific words printed or written on paper, and taped the paper on glass bottles containing untreated, distilled water overnight. They then froze the waters and photographed the molecules using a special microscopic camera. They found that the words caused the formation of either crystalline structures or distorted shapes, depending on the meaning or sentiment conveyed by the words.

The word "love" had a beautifully formed snowflake-like geometric design in a crystalline structure, while the word "hate" had distorted and randomly formed crystalline structures. One interesting observation is that the name of Mother Teresa, the late humanitarian, who was beatified and who some say was the most loving person in the world, formed a beautiful crystalline structure similar to the one formed by the word "love." The crystalline structures formed by classical versus heavy metal music, positive emotions versus negative emotions, and people who exuded love versus those who exuded hatred and megalomania (Adolf Hitler), are quite revealing. They indicate that water is highly responsive to our thoughts, words and emotions. Since water comprises over 70% of the average adult human body, it could be surmised that we can heal and transform our lives with the thoughts we surround ourselves with. More importantly, the study reveals that in the hierarchy of emotions, love (followed by gratitude) is the supreme transformation catalyst of all.

I am certain it has become clear to you that the recurring theme in the above findings is *love*. What is love—and what role does it play in the manifestation of our desires?

Love is a state of *being*, not a state of *feeling*. It goes well beyond the realm of the emotions. It's an attitude of benevolence and kindness towards all creation, including one's self, at all times and under all circumstances.

Love is the most powerful magnetic force in the universe. It is the doorway from the unmanifest to the manifest, and the bridge between the emotional and the spiritual—the pathway from the linear to the non-linear domains. Love is the dynamic force by which the perfection of the physical world was created. Any endeavor that employs the magnetism of love MUST necessarily manifest because love is a vibrational match to God (Divine Source, Universal Mind, Universal Consciousness, Divine Intelligence) — the creative power in all of creation.

When you consider that superior athletes are able to break through barriers of human possibility when motivated by love, so can *you* break through to the unimaginable, indescribable world where effortless creation is a way of life.

The Greatest Manifestation
Principle in the World

Love is the catalyst by which all good things happen. The effortless way to achieve what you desire is to let go of your attachment to results, and focus on love instead. Bring the power of love to your pursuits and to all the people, relationships, resources and events associated with your pursuits. The outcome you get may be different from what you had in mind, but it will be infinitely better than that which you desired.

From the time we're old enough to talk, our parents, society—and the world in general—train us to be results-oriented. We measure our success—and oftentimes our worth—by the results produced by our efforts. Therefore, the majority of us form the lifelong habit of focusing on the results we want, and fail to activate the one thing—*love*—that gives wings to our desires.

That's because we subscribe to the belief that our actions cause results. We do a specific task and we get a specific result. We study hard—and we pass the exam. We send out resumes and go on job interviews—and we get a job. We build a better mousetrap—and the world beats a path to our door. We act, look and behave a certain way, and we attract the attention of the opposite sex. And by extension, we focus on our desires in an effort to trigger manifestation and attract to ourselves the things we want in life.

When your desire is *motivated* by love—and *nourished* by love—it has the highest likelihood of manifestation. The greatest manifestation principle is the process of *co-creating with the divine creative consciousness of love*, the power of which has no equal.

How to Use the Greatest Manifestation Principle to Manifest Your Desires

Step 1: Think about the desires you have at present. Are they motivated by love—or by selfish interests, ambition, revenge, personal gain, or other things? If they are motivated by anything other than love, refine your desire in a way that it becomes an expression of love—perhaps one that is of benefit not just to you, but to others or mankind.

Step 2: Now, think about how you go about the pursuit of your desire. Do you nourish every aspect of your pursuit with love—or do you operate from a spirit of hostile competition, one-upmanship, wrongful pride, exploitation of the weak, shrewdness, control-freakishness or other things? If you're surrounding the pursuit of your desire with anything other than love, change your actions and attitudes to embrace a benevolence and kindness towards everyone you encounter. Think of what you can do to make other people's lives more joyful instead of trying to making them envious of you, or focusing on their usefulness to you. Think of ways of expanding the scope of your pursuit to benefit more people and be of service to mankind. When you encounter conflict or problems, let go of your need to control every situation, your need to win every argument, or your need to be right or appear superior. In every transaction, whether business or personal, ask yourself the question, *'How can I bring love to this interaction?'*

Step 3: Stay connected to the energy field (which is responsible for all of creation, including manifestation) by being in a state of love as often as possible throughout the day. The best way to do this is by practicing the *Love's Pathway* exercise described in Chapter 4, one or more times a day. When the high-frequency vibration of love occupies the same field as lower energies, the lower energies are nullified and transmuted to higher energies.

It is important to emphasize that "connecting to the energy field" does not presuppose that you are not a *part* of the energy field. You are in the field—and it is in you. The only thing that keeps you separate from it, from being one with it, is your identification with your ego. The energy field is not some nebulous, vaporous mass located somewhere outside of you, but rather it is the *totality of creation*, both visible and invisible. Therefore, there is no place you can go, and no step you can take anywhere without being in it. It envelops and enfolds you, and when you shed your ego consciousness, you merge with it. Think of an egg yolk suspended in the albumen (egg white). There is a membrane around the yolk which keeps the yolk separate from the albumen. When you puncture the membrane, the yolk unites with the albumen. The same is true with you, when you take your ego out of the equation, you dissolve into a oneness with the field. When you practice the Love's Pathway exercise, you train yourself to become aware that the field (the divine creative consciousness of love) and you are one.

Think for a moment how your life might change when you follow the 3 steps suggested above. Observe how quickly your desires will manifest when you're in harmony with the universe instead of resisting the natural flow, and separating yourself from others and the world. Notice how joyful the people around you will be and how they will be inclined to contribute to the fulfillment of your desires. Think about how your stress levels will be reduced to a minimum (or to nothing). Imagine how love can enable you to enjoy your life now instead of living for some hoped-for bounty in the uncertain future.

For comparison purposes, consider the above scenario of manifesting versus the way people practice standard manifestation or the Law of Attraction (below): ↓

You have a desire–and you're excited to use the Law of Attraction to manifest it. Chances are, your desire is motivated by personal gain, materialism or some other self-centered pursuit. If your desire happens to be a tangible thing, you cut out a picture of the thing you desire from a magazine or brochure, and you tape it on your bathroom mirror, or wherever you can see it everyday. You visualize your desire often throughout the day. The more you focus on it, the more self-absorbed and emotionally attached you become. Every day, every week and every month that passes by wherein you don't manifest your desire is a reminder of your failure. You don't enjoy the process of being without the thing you desire, so you fantasize about some mind-projected future when you *hope* you will get what you want. After you've given daily visualization and vision boards a fair try and your desire still hasn't manifested, you gradually drop out of the practice. You used to focus on your wants every day, but you cut down to 5 days a week, then 3, then 1, then none. You conclude that the Law of Attraction—or manifestation in general—doesn't work. But you feel it was a personal failure—and the failure weighs heavily on you. People around you feel your low energy and you attract more of it, sending your life into a downward spiral. The failure not only debilitates you, but you're also still without that thing you desire.

Which of the two ways of manifesting described above feels right to you?

I've tried both ways—and the difference is like night and day. Whenever my desire was motivated and nourished by love, I usually manifest not just one but multiple fortunate occurrences or opportunities in a relatively short period of time. One of my experiences was particularly memorable. It occurred in 2009.

A $17,000 Miracle in 7 Days!

In March 2009, my mother's house was in dire need of roof repairs. The house had sentimental value because my late father had designed and built it for our family 40 years earlier. But by 2009, the house was in decrepit shape, and whenever it rained, buckets were placed all over the house to catch the water seeping through the holes in the roof. A roofing contractor, who had been summoned to see what could be done, said that if the roof wasn't fixed immediately, the next time a storm comes, it would come crashing down on its occupants—my mother, sister and her family of 5—and probably kill all of them!

When asked how much it would cost to fix the roof, the contractor replied that it would be $17,000.00. That was an amount that neither I nor my siblings had in our cash reserves because the 2008 meltdown had just adversely affected everyone's incomes. At that time, I was only earning enough to get by—but I already had *The One-Minute Cure* book in circulation. I doubted, though, that I could raise the $17,000 that my mother needed so that she could have her roof fixed before the rains came—and typhoon season was just a month away! I started vigilantly practicing the greatest manifestation principle, being mindful of the doctrine that says, "Any endeavor that is nourished and motivated by love cannot help but succeed."

The very next day after the contractor gave the price quote for the roof repair, something happened that seemed to come like a bolt out of the blue. I received an e-mail from Marcie, a media sales rep, asking if I'd be interested in advertising *The One-Minute Cure* book to the 100,000 subscribers of their health newsletter. She said it would cost $6,500 to send out our e-mail ad to the 100,000 subscribers. I felt that the price was quite steep, considering the possibility that sales of the book from that e-mail promotion may not even be enough to cover the cost of the ad. But something inside me felt that this was a message from divine intelligence—the field of Infinite Potentiality—that could be the solution to the roof problems of my mom's house.

I decided to trust in the universe so I paid the $6,500 advertising fee using a credit card—and the e-mail ad promoting *The One-Minute Cure* book was broadcast on 2 consecutive days, March 26 and 27. Sales of the book began to come in, and 5 days later, I calculated the net profits from the book by taking the Gross Profit generated in those 5 days and deducting the $6,500 ad cost. **The net profits came to $17,000—the exact amount my mother needed to have her roof fixed!** If that's not a manifestation miracle, I don't know what is!

I sent the $17,000 to my mother immediately, not keeping even a cent for myself. My mother wept because she had been praying for a miracle like this, never imagining that it would come just 7 days after the contractor inspected her house. The roof repairs were done within 2 weeks, and the biggest miracle was just about to make itself known.

One week after the roof repair was done, the biggest typhoon to hit the city in 20 years came down with a vengeance, leaving devastation and countless dead people in its wake. There was no doubt that her house would have crumbled beneath the weight of that typhoon—had her roof not been repaired in the nick of time. My mother's house—and the lives of everyone who lived under her roof—were saved!

And if that were the end of the story, it would have already been a wonderful testament to the power of the greatest manifestation principle—love. But the story was far from over. I'm convinced that as a result of that pivotal moment, a cascade of fortuitous events happened. *The One-Minute Cure* hit its highest single-month sales of $246,000 the following month (April 2009), and the book became the Amazon No. 1 bestselling book in the Health, Body and Mind category for the first time that same month—the first of 15 more times to come over the next 6 years. And that was the start of *The One-Minute Cure* book's skyrocketing into the stratosphere, which ultimately generated a cumulative $7 million in revenue.

While *The One-Minute Cure* and my 3 business enterprises were making millions of dollars in sales, I made it a point to give away between 60% to 75% of my annual income to family members, friends, charities, and people who I felt could use a helping hand. Because this act of giving was nourished and motivated by love, the money kept coming back to me ten-fold or more.

The above example illustrates clearly that love is not just something you can apply towards the manifestation of your desires. Whenever you exercise love and kindness towards others—even when it has nothing to do with your desires—the universe has a way of rewarding you by looking after your needs. Notice, too, that I was not focusing on my desires at all, but instead I had let go of my desires, trusting that the universe would provide what I desired.

When you live your life from the standpoint of being of benefit or service to others or mankind (instead of selfish interests)—or operate from the premise of supporting life and all creation—the universe will respond with ways to benefit and support you.

Love's rewards are beyond comprehension, and are usually much more than one had hoped for or imagined—and sometimes it isn't always what you focus on that will yield the fulfillment of your desires. Sometimes, the rewards come from the most unexpected sources. This is true, too, when it comes to people who are the recipients of your love and kindness—they will not necessarily be the ones to reciprocate or reward you. Acts of love and kindness have no boundaries, and their rewards often don't come from where you expect them to originate.

It should be noted that the concept of love, as presented here, is a way for you to **be**—as opposed to merely a way for you to act, look or behave. When you give full expression to your loving nature, people around you will also be positively influenced to give full expression to their loving nature towards you—not through your prompting but as a consequence of being in your vicinity. You attract to yourself that which you emanate. When you remove the obstacles to the awareness of love's presence within you, it becomes easy to love yourself and others as well. When you love yourself, you project that love upon the world. The more you love yourself, the more loving your world becomes—and you begin to experience a reality of your own creation.

> "We don't see things as *they* are. We see them as *we* are.
> – Anais Nin

Love is—and has always been—the most powerful currency of the world. Yet, only a small percentage of people in this world live by the principle of love. All the great spiritual leaders of the world have embraced this principle and called it "the way" to ultimate fulfillment.

Instead, the majority of us still live our lives without using this principle. Interestingly enough, other self-improvement disciplines often advise us to do something contrary to this greatest manifestation principle—advocating the focus on results instead of love.

While there's nothing intrinsically wrong with focusing on the things you want in life—and getting your desires so clear that you can almost see them, smell them, hear, touch and feel them—the current standard teachings on manifestation and the Law of Attraction fail to mention what it is that takes those desires from their unformed potentiality to physical actuality—and that is, love.

Visualizing and affirming your desires without adding love to the equation is akin to a rocket that doesn't have sufficient propulsion to catapult it into space.

I've no doubt the people who have managed to succeed by focusing on their desires must have unwittingly fueled their intentions with love somewhere along the way. If they didn't put love in the equation and still managed to make a fortune, one has to wonder how much larger a fortune they might have made if they did focus on love.

The same holds true when it comes to relationships. Some couples manage to make their relationship work by going through the motions—and even when they're driven by selfish motives and not by love. But one has to wonder how much more blissful their relationship could be if they made love the focus of their relationship.

Positive Thoughts Are Not All Created Equal

If you're like most people who practice standard manifestation or the Law of Attraction, the first thing you learned was that thinking positive thoughts is the best way to attract positive things that are a vibrational match to your thoughts. You've been taught to acquire the habit of thinking of things that make you feel good, and replacing a negative thought with a positive thought (flip-switching) the moment you sense a negative thought arising. The positive thought could be anything from picturing a giggling baby, to visualizing yourself enjoying a vacation at your favorite destination, to feeling the exhilaration of seeing a rainbow after a storm—or anything that gives you those warm, fuzzy feelings.

One thing I noticed is that most people don't make any differentiation between the positive thoughts or feelings they generate—seldom favoring one over another, and usually using whatever thought or feeling is easiest to manufacture at will. Sometimes, for variety, people even mix up the positive thoughts—or rotate all of them just to cover all the bases. But in so doing, they often pay little attention to—or ignore altogether—the *one* positive thought (love) that really makes the big difference.

Ultimately, the results they get are usually diluted—either they manifest their desires sporadically with no consistency whatsoever, or they don't manifest their desires at all. Is it any wonder why those who practice the standard manifestation or the Law of Attraction get more misses than hits as far as the manifestation of their desires are concerned?

You see, positive thoughts and feelings are not all created equal. Just thinking of something pleasurable or delightful creates vibrations of a lower frequency than love because those thoughts and feelings are self-oriented (receiving) whereas love is outwardly-oriented (giving). Consider the athletes mentioned in the beginning of this chapter. When they held in mind selfish motives for winning—even when that motive was accompanied by positive thoughts of becoming a star or making a lot of money— they tested weak in the muscle test. When they held in mind noble motives such as the dedication of their performance to someone they love or for the love of their country, or viewed their athletic performance as a gift to mankind, they tested strong, excelled in athletic events, and sometimes even broke through a performance barrier to a new level of human possibility.

One might conclude that giving, not getting, is the key to true achievement and the manifestation of desires. This is not to say that people have never been known to achieve things through selfish ambition. Yes, they have. However, rarely does achievement derived from selfish aims ever produce an enduring sense of accomplishment and joy.

Suffice it to say, therefore, that in the pursuit of your desires, ascend to the level of love before choosing any other positive thoughts and feelings. Love's Pathway as described in Chapter 4, will help you accomplish this. Love has the vibrational power against which all other positive thoughts and feelings pale by comparison.

The Undercurrent of All Your Activities

As previously mentioned, it is possible to generate some results by being results-oriented instead of focusing on love. However, it's worthwhile to ask the question: *What results are you not getting because you didn't apply the greatest manifestation principle in the pursuit of your goals?*

When you switch your focus to love instead of desires, and allow love to be the undercurrent of all your activities …

… you will free yourself from past concerns and wasteful preoccupations

… your creativity becomes fully expressed

… you gain a charisma to which people are magnetically drawn

… your entire outlook on life and relationships will improve

… you will gain excellence in any field of human endeavor that you choose

… you will spontaneously attract people who are like-minded and who will be instrumental in the fulfillment of your desires

… you will be able to easily let go of the non-essential and deleterious things in your life; and

… you will raise the energy level of anyone in your vicinity.

"If you gain the world and all its bounty, but have no love, your life is but a dance without a soul, a song without a heart, or a prayer without devotion."
— Carnelian Sage

A desire that is motivated by a higher principle, such as love, peace, loyalty, dedication to God, truth or country, is a desire whose manifestation brings great spiritual upliftment. The greatest of those higher principles is love. Those who acquire things in their life through the use of force, or by operating from anything other than love or other life-enhancing principles, get results that have no spiritual merit—and the pleasure derived from them is short-lived like the 'high" derived from a drug.

Knowing this, how might your life change if, instead of focusing on worldly pursuits that are ephemeral and transient, you began focusing on love, which has eternal value?

A sequoia seed in your hand has the potential to become a giant sequoia tree. But it's not a giant sequoia tree yet. It's only a seed in your hand. You cannot *cause* it to become a giant sequoia tree, even if you spent your whole life visualizing that it is a giant sequoia tree. But what you can do is provide the *conditions* in which the seed's potentiality comes into manifestation. Just add fertile soil, sunshine and rain—and just like clockwork it will grow into a giant tree, perhaps reaching a height of 350 to 400 feet like some of the tallest sequoias in the world. The seed becomes a tree because of the creative *power of the energy* field that allows the seed's unformed potential to manifest into actuality. Likewise, your desire is much like a seed in your hand. You cannot *cause* it to transform itself from a desire to the actualization of that desire unless you provide the *conditions* in which its potentiality comes into manifestation. The major condition necessary for that to happen is love. Other conditions, such as the positive thoughts, feelings and visualization do help, but the actualization of your desire will be stunted and will never grow to the highest of its potential without love. Therefore, nourish your desire with love and imbue everything around it with the power of devotion.

> "It is not how much you do, but how much Love you put into the doing that matters." — Mother Teresa

Although love is the most powerful ingredient for manifesting desires, it is hoped that this application of it does not become a mere means to an end. Instead, endeavor to love because you want to love—because it is the full expression of God in you. Love because you *get to* love—it is a privilege, not an obligation. And finally, love because you can never be more like God than when you love other human beings for love's own sake.

To love is to live.

Chapter 4

Entering the Realm of Miracles

"Miracles occur naturally as expressions of love. The real miracle is the love that inspires them. In this sense everything that comes from love is a miracle."— Excerpt from *A Course in Miracles*

Love is not just something you *do*. It's what you *are*.

Most people live their lives in a state of oblivious slumber, never awakening to the realization of this spiritual truth.

As explained in the previous chapter, love is the attitude of benevolence, reverence and kindness for all creation, including one's self, at all times and under all circumstances.

Every man, woman and child has love at the core of their being. It's every person's natural inheritance. If you believe in the premise that you are made in the image and likeness of God, then just as God is love, so are you. And so is every human being in the world.

Contrary to what most people might think, and what Webster's dictionary says, love is not an emotion or a feeling. Neither is it a commodity that you give to another human being or receive from another human being. Neither is it something that you can create or extinguish. Rather, love is the essence of who you are. It is something you embody as a human being. More than the flesh and bones that comprise your body, more than the blood coursing through your veins, and more than the 6,000 miles of neurons wired throughout your body, you are—first and foremost—love.

A human being is often compared to a computer. The person's essential nature, which is love, is the computer hardware. This hardware never changes, no matter what software runs on it. The programs that are installed in that hardware by society, upbringing, education, experience and everything else, are the software. The software is what's running in the forefront, and the computer begins to be identified with the programs it runs (what it can *do*) and not its hardware (what it *is*). But the nature of the hardware is not affected—it just runs quietly in the background.

It's the same thing with human beings. Love is their true nature—but because they're programmed by the things of the world, you only see what they *do* and not who they *are*.

A human being's nature (love) remains unblemished, no matter what behavior they display—no matter what actions they take, what thoughts they think or what words they speak. They still remain as love in disguise.

Knowing this, it should become easier for you to discern the inherent beauty that resides within each person. When they hurt you, offend you and take advantage of you, you'll know that it's a result of the programs they're running and you're able to forgive them for they're unaware that they're acting unconsciously, oblivious of their true nature.

At some point, a computer could be corrupted by the programs that are running on it, or by other extraneous variables. It then needs to be reformatted, and when that happens and all the programs are removed, the computer is again restored to its original, untarnished state. Likewise, human beings can get corrupted by the complexities of society and life in the modern world, but they can easily return to their original, untainted state of love when they choose to abandon their attachments to the ego and things that are obstacles to the realization of their true self. These attachments include fear, doubt, worry, anxiety, hatred, resentment, envy, stress, depression—and anything that does not foster love, joy and peace.

Love is clearly something awesome embodying every person that is far greater than the genetic information stored in the DNA, which resides in the nucleus of each human cell. Some refer to it as the vast intelligence that comprises our entire being, and some call it energy. Indeed, love is energy in its most fundamental sense— the raw material of all that is. It's the most profoundly essential and transformative energy, without which life itself would not be possible.

The loving nature of humans is a demonstrable fact. If you were to put two people, both strangers to each other, alone on a deserted island—they will eventually come to love each other. It's simply the nature of human beings to have the innate tendency and capacity to love.

But what about sociopaths, serial killers, wife beaters, child molesters, rapists, criminals, megalomaniacs or bigots who seem to be full of hatred, or show the desire to harm others or themselves—how could they possibly have a loving nature? They don't appear to have love because there are obstacles that prevent them from perceiving or expressing their essential nature, which is love. *Removing the blocks to their awareness of love's presence within them* is the key to creating dramatic transformations in their lives.

Likewise, if you're motivated by, or operating on things other than love, you simply have obstacles that keep you from seeing your loving nature. Love is like a bright sun that shines ceaselessly within you, and you just have to remove the clouds that hide its dazzling light. Love is the natural state that prevails when *fear*—and the other *obstacles* that prevent one from perceiving or expressing one's essential loving nature—are eradicated.

When you give *full expression* to the love that resides within, you unleash an *immeasurable power* and an *irresistible influence* that knows no bounds.

The *irony* of it all is that we as human beings have lost touch with that nature. We think love is just something we do, or something we give and receive, and not something **we are**. As a result, almost all our desires and aspirations center on *getting love*.

Consider why a person would want to lose weight— usually it's because they want to look good. Why do they want to look good? Because they want to gain the approval or admiration of others—or themselves. When you break their motives down further, you arrive at the one core reason why they do what they do. It's because deep down, what they truly want is love. They want other people to love them—and they want to love themselves.

The same holds true of our desire for success or wealth. Our desire for them all boils down to our need for love. And that's where the irony lies because as human beings, we already embody that which we seek—because we **are** love. Not just a doer of love, or a recipient of love, but a *being* of love.

Love's Pathway

Being in a state of love is an absolute necessity if you want to be connected to the energy field which is responsible for the fulfillment of desires. The quality of *being loving* is not the same as *being love*, and neither does it have the same effect.

You might say that some of the most loving people that you've ever known hardly manifest their desires or live the good life. It's important to note that just because people seem loving doesn't mean they are in harmony with the energy field. They may display the *outward appearance* of lovingness, but it's possible that their loving behavior is motivated by insecurity, fear, a desperate need to be loved, pity, manipulation or control of others, to extract reciprocity or gain favor, or a host of other things that have nothing to do with love. There are also some people who are masters at the conspicuous display of generosity and kindness, which may be done for the admiration and applause of people—and not born out of genuine love. And then, of course, there are those who are fundamentally loving, but their prevalent thoughts center on low-energy emotions such as shame, anger, guilt, fear, frustration, resentment or judgment. In all of these cases, the individual is not *being* love but simply *going through the motions* of love, thereby never really connecting to the energy field.

The best way to connect to the energy field and remove the obstacles to the awareness of love's presence within one's self, is by doing the *powerful* exercise featured below called **Love's Pathway**. Love's Pathway is the way to connect, resonate, and vibrate to the divine creative consciousness of love, with which you *co-create through intention*. Your intention is to consciously connect to the consciousness of love in every moment.

1) Close your eyes and breathe deeply 3 or 4 times, while saying the following to yourself: *I am the full expression of God's love. Just as God is love, so am I. I am love.*

2) Hold in mind the image of someone you love. This could be a family member, a spouse, boyfriend, girlfriend or significant other. Then imagine yourself putting your arms around that person in a loving embrace while simultaneously saying "I love you" in your mind. Hold on to this feeling of love, allowing it to spread throughout your entire being.

3) While holding on to this feeling of love, silently say to yourself, "I feel love." After a few moments mentally say, "I feel God." Then finally, in your mind say, "Thank you," allowing the feeling of gratitude and appreciation to wash over you.

4) Remain in this state of *being* love for a few minutes, imagining the love in you radiating outward in an egg-

shaped sphere of vibratory energy that flows out onto all people, encompassing the world and the universe.

You may repeat the process, holding in mind the image of another loved one in the next cycle, and still another loved one in another cycle. Or you may want to do, as I do—and practice several cycles, going through every member of your family in succession.

The profound effect of the above exercise cannot be emphasized enough. It may seem disarmingly simple, but it awakens in you feelings you didn't know you had. You'll learn the secrets of your heart, and the extent to which you can love another human being, and truly love yourself. It will also magnify the love that you already have for those you love, and create a deeper bond between you and them.

Allow me to walk you through the various stages of the exercise, and what each step accomplishes.

1) When you breathe deeply 3 or 4 times, this enables you to *center yourself*, silence your mind, and remove all extraneous thoughts and feelings in preparation for the exercise. As you contemplate on the truth that you, as a human being, are the full expression of God's love, you gain a newfound view of yourself that defies description. Whatever labels your ego may have imposed on you in the past, you now have the proper label, and that is ... you are love. It's your essence and your identity. You'll feel a

dismantling of your self-imposed imprisonment of pride and the ego-based emotions of resentment, fear, doubt, worry, greed or hatred.

2) When you hold in mind the image of someone you love, this immediately puts your body in a state of strength. The science of applied kinesiology, pioneered by Dr. George Goodheart in the latter part of the 20th century, shows through muscle testing that certain stimuli increase the strength of certain indicator muscles while other stimuli would cause those same muscles to weaken. Emotional stimuli, such as picturing someone you love, provokes a demonstrably strong muscle response when compared to negative or neutral stimuli. According to the late Dr. David Hawkins's Map of Consciousness®, the emotional state of love registers as one of the highest levels of consciousness.

3) When you imagine putting your arms around a loved one while at the same time silently saying, "I love you", and then allowing the feeling of love to spread throughout your entire being, this act of loving another human being allows you to spontaneously detach from your identification with the ego because you're focusing on your loved one. Since, at that very moment, you're loving someone without condition or expectation of reciprocity, you step outside of yourself and transcend the ego for the time being.

At this stage, when you're in the emotional state of love, it's not unusual for oxytocin levels in your body to more than double. Oxytocin is a hormone produced by the hypothalamus and released by the pituitary into the bloodstream. It's often called the love chemical. It's impossible to hold a grudge when oxytocin levels are elevated naturally or via pharmaceutical oxytocin. That's because it activates the body's natural tendency to forgive—without consciously trying to forgive. And this could be the beginning of unconditional love.

Different people have different triggers that cause them to have deep feelings of love. Many of us respond to the sense of touch—therefore, envisioning a loving embrace or a gentle caress is just the key. For others, the deepest feeling of love is triggered when they say or hear the words, "I love you." In this step, feel free to add whatever it is that causes you to have deep feelings of love.

This is the emotional phase of the exercise. It allows you to start with the *feelings* of love that you're already familiar with, and use them as a *catalyst* for accessing the deeper dimensions of love that reside within you.

4) When you say to yourself, "I feel love" it brings crystal clear realization that something inside of you— your true loving nature—is finding full expression. Once you feel love, your individual consciousness of love connects to and merges with the greater all-encompassing consciousness of love, which is the field of all potentialities. At this stage, you are accessing the creative energy source—the field of

creation where all the subtle energy resources that you need to co-create your physical reality are located.

When you say, "I feel God," a shift in awareness occurs as you realize you've found the bridge—the "wormhole", if you will—between emotional and spiritual dimensions, and you've opened the doorway to God through love.

When you say, "Thank you" it is an expression of profound gratitude and appreciation for the spiritual vision to see who you really are, and to revel in your boundless capacity to love. Gratitude is also the ultimate state of receptiveness to accept the manifestation of your desires before they have actually manifested. It's a state of *trust and readiness to receive* what the universe has in store for you.

The ultimate objective of doing the Love's Pathway exercise regularly is that you raise your frequency of vibration so that it ultimately becomes a vibrational match to the energy field, which means you've realigned yourself with the field.

Quantum physicists theorize that consciousness evolves and expands through feedback. Consciousness is self-learning, self-organizing, self-observing, and constantly evolving. It expands and continuously evolves from all experiential input in an informational exchange. Therefore, the more the consciousness of love dwells in us, the more expansive the divine creative consciousness of love becomes. When we feel love, we merge into a oneness with love—and we *become love*, which is an aspect of divinity. The more we remain in the state of being love, the more love is available and accessible for us to co-create our reality.

Conscious connection to the energy field can happen in a *split second*. Many people are able to catch glimpses of this connection for brief moments—or maybe a few minutes, hours or days—when they are in an altered state of consciousness, or when they are experiencing a spiritual epiphany or a religious experience. It's characterized by that sublime, surreal feeling that everything is right in the world, that one has access to all the wisdom in the universe, and that anything one sets out to do will meet with success.

While it's wonderful to experience that euphoric feeling of being connected, unless you can sustain that state longer than just a momentary period, it's nothing more than a spiritual "high" that will do little towards the fulfillment of your heart's desires. When you awaken to the full realization that *you are love*, and practice the *Love's Pathway* exercise regularly, you *perpetuate* that state—and it becomes the "normal cruising altitude" of your life. That's when miracles begin to happen, and you experience the definition of self-realization referred to by Swami

Paramananda, as follows: "Self-realization means that we have been consciously connected with our source of being. Once we have made this connection, then nothing can go wrong."

There are many ways of arriving at that conscious connection with the energy field. Often, it takes a lifetime of spiritual agony and suffering, combined with the performance of traditional spiritual practices. Consciously connecting with the energy field by doing Love's Pathway is the *accelerated* method—the sudden emergence into higher awareness, which dramatically shortens the time it takes to manifest desires.

When you merge into a oneness with love, everything in your reality resides within the creative consciousness of love. Think of this consciousness as a boundless sphere encompassing and permeating all facets, all aspects and dimensions of your reality—which include your loved ones, your career, your house, your life partner, your health, and even your unmanifested desires waiting to manifest into your reality. In this state of being, there is no need for you to "send" love or "send" healing energy to someone you love. You just need to *be* love, and that love energy you radiate connects you to the field—the same field that the person you love is a part of.

One practical method that can enhance and accelerate your conscious connection with the energy field is by listening to frequencies—such as the 528 Hz, which corresponds to the frequency of love. In the discussion of the Map of Consciousness® (Chapter 2), the Emotional Frequency Chart allows you to identify the emotional state you're in at any given moment. Most people who are operating at ordinary levels of awareness are in the emotional states of shame, guilt, fear, anger or one of the states vibrating between 1 Hz to 200 Hz. A simple shift in frequency can bring you from your current emotional state to the higher frequency of love by listening to an audio of the love frequency (500 Hz and above). You'll effectively bypass the lower levels of consciousness and go straight to the level of Love where your body will be vibrating at 500 Hz or above within a few minutes. This will then put you in the creative level of consciousness which is the ideal springboard for manifestation. [There are many audio files available at YouTube.com. Just type "love frequency 528 Hz" in the search box.]

When you cast a pebble of love in the ocean of life, the ripples you create will return to you in waves, according to your heart's desires. If you cast no pebbles, there will be no waves to propel your heart's desires and enable them to arrive at your shores.

I'll never forget the first time I did the Love's Pathway

exercise. It was just before I went to bed on a week night. As I went about picturing my loved ones, tears streamed down my face continuously as I beheld the true beauty of love. I had thought myself a loving person prior to the exercise, but that night, in just a few minutes, I experienced a spectacular breakthrough, more profound than anything I had previously known. There simply was nothing in my ordinary existence that compared to it. I emerged from the exercise with the infinite presence of an exquisite peace and a brand new pair of eyes—eyes that saw in each person, beneath imperfect appearances, the shining magnificence of love and beauty. I became convinced I had become another person altogether—and that I had arrived at an enlightened sphere of consciousness, where I was at once the lover and the loved. I realized this place was the rarefied air of the quantum field, Source Energy, the field of all possibilities—of God—with which I had become one. I finally understood that this place inside of me is where truth prevails—and where God lives. I knew then that all things were, are, and will always be possible for me.

I experienced a previously unattained level of spiritual awareness upon the very first practice, and have only become better with each succeeding session of Love's Pathway. It should be noted that every advanced spiritual seeker knows that at certain levels of spiritual awareness, physical diseases spontaneously become healed and pain instantly disappears. There is no scientific explanation for this—it's simply an awe-inspiring phenomenon.

Love, in this context, doesn't simply mean other people's love for you (although the love of other people is often a catalyst in healing). It doesn't imply sitting around passively waiting for someone to love you. It actually refers to your own capacity to love—and this comes from removing the obstacles to the awareness of love's presence within yourself. When those obstacles are removed, one discovers a deep and abiding love and reverence for one's self, as well as for others. This spiritual love, then, goes beyond emotion and beyond the outward appearance of lovingness—but is rather a state of being "in love"—being within the divine matrix of love. It is not dependent on someone else's love for you. If people love you, that's wonderful—but if they don't, you find it in yourself to love them anyway. As your spiritual awareness grows, you begin to discover that "being loved" goes beyond having someone love you, and even beyond loving yourself—but it is an energy that you are a part of—the same energy that created the universe and everything that's in it. Ultimately, you realize that this energy field of inexhaustible love is within you—and within you also resides the source of your happiness.

When you become connected to this inexhaustible supply of love, you're not only able to heal yourself but also heal other people who are unable to heal themselves. Sometimes, all that is necessary to heal another person is just to love them at the spiritual level. You connect to the loving essence of the ill person and allow them to heal by their own recognition that they are loved. One should not attempt to do this in place of necessary medical attention, however, and before an adequate level of spiritual awareness has been achieved.

"Where there is great love, there are always miracles."
– Willa Cather

The opposite of love is not hatred. It is *fear*. Love is the natural state of being when fear is eradicated. Conversely, fear is the most common obstacle that keeps us from being aware of love's presence within us. The *Love's Pathway* exercise helps tremendously in removing fear because fear is simply an ego-based emotion, and consistent practice of the *Love's Pathway* exercise allows one to transcend the ego.

When you transcend fear, love becomes as effortless as a spacecraft breaking through the earth's gravitational field and finding itself floating in the sublime weightlessness of outer space. The accompanying state of bliss is not unlike the feeling of one's self dissolving into a oneness with God and with all creation. Love goes far beyond the realm that the mind can comprehend, and enters into the domain of the spirit.

The ideal place for you to practice the *Love's Pathway* exercise is anywhere you can step away from the hustle and bustle of the world, and have some peace and quiet without interruptions. However, you may also practice short sessions anytime throughout the day, whenever you have a minute or two, even while standing in line at the supermarket or the post office, or in between repetitions at the gym. The more often you practice it, the better. This has a compounding effect.

When you practice *Love's Pathway* on the people you love, have no desire but to love them for love's own sake. Let go of your need to manipulate or control their thinking, feelings or attitudes, and relinquish your desire to have them adjust themselves to make you happy. Just surround them with an unconditional love that requires no reciprocity. You'll begin to witness miracles happening when you let go of your attachment to the outcome produced by your love.

If the spirit moves you, you may even want to practice *Love's Pathway* on total strangers that you meet on the street, or anyone who you think is in need of love, such as a family member with whom you have a strained relationship, a rude waitress, your mean boss, a vindictive rival, or that condescending mom in your child's soccer team. The rewards are endless when you make love a habit that you do all day long. You'll also find that miracles will become an everyday occurrence.

You'll know you've fully unmasked your true loving nature when you begin to see the world and everything in it as being beautiful. This means you've seen within yourself the beauty of who you are—the beauty of love. You project onto the world what you see inside.

When you *are* love, your world is simply a reflection of what you've become.

Chapter 5

How to Infuse Your Life with the Greatest Manifestation Principle

1) Cultivating the Most Important Relationship of All

Some people consider a loving relationship with their spouse, child, parent, friend, family member, boyfriend/ girlfriend—or the current object of their affection—their primary relationship. But there is an even more important relationship that needs to be developed before you can expect your relationships with other people to be truly fruitful and free of conflict. That is the relationship you have with yourself.

Your relationship with yourself directs the course and determines the success or failure of your relationships with other people. In cultivating a relationship with yourself, because your true self is love, you are developing a deep connection with the source of love, which is God (whom I've referred to as the energy field throughout this book). Therefore, endeavor to consciously connect with your source of being so that your vibrational energy matches up to that of God from whom all good things come.

You cannot discover in another person what you can't first discover in yourself. Whatever you perceive in yourself is what you project upon other people, and by extension, the world. If you see imperfection in others, you haven't been made perfect in love. You know you've found beauty and love in yourself only when you see beauty and love in all people, including those who might appear unattractive to others and those who are unlovable.

You can find beauty and love in yourself by moving yourself into the field of awareness that you are love. The Love's Pathway exercise can help you accomplish this. Knowing your true identity is one of the most life-altering realizations you will ever have in your life. The pure, resplendent joy of being love, and the profound peace that accompanies it, is your true wealth.

Extend your love upon your circle of family, friends and acquaintances, and let it expand to everyone you meet or interact with in your community and the world. Show kindness towards all of life in all of its expressions, including yourself. Be willing to forgive yourself and other people, and endeavor to perceive each person as having the same loving nature as you. Practice loving those who have hurt or offended you or caused you to experience suffering. When you are able to love all people and all things, you become love, and you attract to yourself all good things that are a vibrational match to love.

2) Surrendering to the Divine

Accessing your true self may prove to be difficult when the challenges of life and ego-based emotions get in the way. Ease comes when you surrender every aspect of yourself to the divine. When you do this, you'll experience a significant shift in your personal world and the world at large.

Surrender not only your pain, suffering, resentment, anger, self-pity, grief, victimization, the feeling of being wronged, being offended, being cheated on, being taken advantage of—but also your personal agenda and your desires—as they arise. Surrender the way you see things and trust that when you remain consciously connected with the energy field (God), you will perceive a more magnificent view of the world than you've ever seen, and gain access to the infinite power of the energy field.

Let go of all resistance to the flow of life. Your job is to be in harmony at all times with the energy field through love. When you impose your standards, expectations and preconceived notions on what and how the universe will deliver its bounty to you, you virtually set up barriers that keep you from getting all the good things the energy field has in store for you.

Above all, surrender your fears whenever they arise. Fear is a denial of the existence of the divine power that resides within you—the divine power of which you are a part. And fear is the low energy that obscures the presence of love. Be willing to step away from the ego-based emotion of fear, as well as everything that stands in the way of your awareness of the divinity that lives in you. Escaping to the realm of love will not only restore your energy, but also bring you immense peace.

It is human nature to take a position on anything—or labeling anything as either good or bad, healthy or unhealthy, or something being this as opposed to that. The moment you label a person, event, circumstance or thing as being a certain way, you set up a reaction to it. For example, if you label an event as disappointing, you instantly assume the position of resisting the disappointment. It's the way you've labeled it—and the accompanying resistance—that causes something to be experienced as disappointing. The moment you surrender your position, let go of your resistance and consciously connect to the energy field, that person, event, circumstance or thing ceases to be disappointing. The source of the disappointment stems from the way you see things and label things. With constant surrender, however, virtually all human dilemmas and all things that you regard as undesirable—including illness, lack, hostility, heartbreak and other challenging issues—vanish and your life becomes transformed.

3) Everything is As It Should Be

In the quest to manifest our desires, we often demand

that the world—and all the people and things in it—be different from what they presently are. We want things to change in order to suit our purposes and fit our idea of order and perfection—so we try to fix the world and control others in order to accomplish it. This constitutes resistance to the flow of the universe.

You make a difference in your world not by trying to fix things according to your wishes and specifications. At any given moment, everything is as it should be, based on the energy you've sown or not sown. Therefore, there's no sense in resisting the way things are. Instead, the way to make the biggest impact on your world is by focusing your efforts on raising your own level of consciousness, being in touch with your true self and being connected to the Source. Doing so frees up your energy from wasteful preoccupations and enables you to use it for creative purposes. It also allows the energy of the universe to flow—unimpeded by your resistance.

With the exception of children, who rightfully need to be trained until they reach the age of self-sufficiency, let go of your desire to change people to suit your purposes. Accept the fact that you cannot make people do something they're not naturally predisposed to doing, nor can you cause them to become anyone other than who they are. To do so would entail the use of threat, demands, punishment, manipulation, persuasion or other devices that employ some manner of control or force. There are psychological principles and relationship strategies that might seem to produce behavioral modifications in people, but those changes are not likely to last if they're not tied to the true nature of people.

We, as human beings, tend to view other people merely as a means to our desired ends—as though they existed solely to serve our purposes. Love is often so glaringly absent in our interactions with people, and we focus instead on how well (or how poorly) our own needs are being met—seldom thinking about the human beings with whom we are interacting, and seldom caring about them more than we care about ourselves.

Endeavor to hold all people you encounter in the highest regard—not because of what you hope they can do for you, nor the needs you hope they can meet, or for any reason other than just because you behold their magnificence as spiritual beings whom you treasure and love far beyond what you perceive as their usefulness to you. Let every thought of them, every word you speak to them, and everything you do for them and with them become imbued with love

Again, the only way you can make an important difference in people's lives is by moving yourself into the field of awareness that you are love, and by removing all the obstacles which keep you from identifying yourself as being love. Love must begin as a flame that you reignite within yourself before you can influence others to reignite it within themselves.

4) The World's Rules of Economy Do Not Apply

The world's rules of economy are based on the exchange of goods and services. Each party in a transaction brings goods, services or funds to the table, and each receives something in return that represents a fair and equitable exchange. Because this model works very well in most instances, we often try to apply the fairness principle on our relationships. More often than not, this becomes the source of a relationship problem. Two people in a relationship rarely contribute an equal amount of time, resources or devotion to a relationship, and when this inequity happens, someone ends up feeling shortchanged, resentment builds, and discord results. "But that's not fair!" and "What about my needs?" become common anthems. The ego rears its head, and the individuals involved in a relationship begin to entertain feelings of being taken for granted, being used, being wronged—and other expressions of being offended.

Love's economy doesn't operate in this kind of give-and-take relay. If it did, love wouldn't endure. If the love of a mother for her infant child depended on what the infant contributed to the mother-child relationship, there would be no such thing as motherly love. By the same token, if the love of a woman for a man depended on whether a man fulfilled her needs or not, there will oftentimes be a deficit—either real or imagined—from the woman's viewpoint. The fulfillment of needs has never been, nor will it ever be, the ideal standard for perpetuating love in a relationship.

In our narcissistic culture, it is often difficult to view another person's "reality" as being just as important as our own. We tend to focus on what we are getting, how we are being treated, and what's in it for us—and we usually perceive other people's lives in terms of how they affect our own lives. Develop the practice of focusing on other people instead. What can you do to add to their well-being, or make their lives more joyful? This practice enables you to step outside of yourself, and want just as much for other people as you want for yourself—or more. This is the beginning of true power.

The bottom line is that one cannot use the world's rules of economy—nor can you use psychology or any standards of the physical world—to govern something that does not belong in the physical or mental realm. Love belongs in the realm of the soul.

Love is complete in and of itself, lacking nothing—and requiring nothing from that which it loves. Therein lies another important distinction between the world view and the spiritual view. The world sees a relationship as being successful when the needs of both parties in the relationship are mutually fulfilled. "You give me what I need, and I give you what you need." Quid pro quo. Unconditional love, on the other hand, needs nothing but to seek the full expression of itself.

5) The Key to Happiness

In a previous chapter, I mentioned that the best way to have your desires fulfilled is to let go of those desires. According to kinesiological muscle testing, being in a state of desire weakens a person. Desire ranks 6th to the lowest among the levels of enlightenment in the Map of Consciousness® developed by David Hawkins, MD, PhD— even lower than pride and anger. It calibrates below the level of neutrality, together with other weakening, low-frequency emotions such as shame, guilt, apathy, grief and fear.

Inherent in every desire is the unconscious belief that the fulfillment of the desire will bring you happiness. This belief makes you dependent on external conditions—and therefore, you're always in a weak and vulnerable position, always fearful that your happiness is at the whim of something or someone else. If, instead, you strive for self-fulfillment through conscious connection with the energy field, which is the source of all things, then no one can take your happiness away from you.

Let go of the state of "wanting" and be in the state of "having" or "accepting" instead. The only reason you desire something is because you think you can find happiness outside of yourself. If you get your dream car, then you'll feel proud driving it around, then you'll feel happy. If you get a dream job, you'll feel successful, then you'll feel happy. If you win the lottery, you'll be rich, then you'll be happy.

This illusion of happiness seems true only because we're conditioned to define happiness through external conditions like luck, good fortune, or the favor or approval we receive from people. It even infiltrates the language we use in our everyday lives. We say things like, "I'm so happy that my boss gave me a raise," or "My husband/wife makes me so happy" or "Owning my dream house makes me happy" or "Being successful in my chosen career makes me happy." These statements presuppose that something outside of ourselves makes us happy when in actuality, it is how we represent the event, person, or circumstance to our own mind that brought about the state of happiness.

> "We represent the world to ourselves and respond to our representations."
> – *The Crack in the Cosmic Egg*, Joseph Chilton Pearce

Happiness is not an emotion that is caused by people, events or circumstances. It is a state that we choose to create in ourselves, sometimes as a result of people, events and circumstances. We've been conditioned to rely on external things to make us happy, when in fact, we don't have to wait for them to happen to us in order to be happy. Since we already know that happiness is something we choose to create, based on how we represent circumstances to our own mind, it stands to reason that you can choose to create happiness anytime, without waiting for luck or good fortune to come around, or before your desires are manifested.

Ultimately, it is you and you alone who can make yourself happy. This is true of all negative emotional states as well—you alone can make yourself become fearful, anxious, doubtful, stressed out or full of worry. You choose to create them within yourself, or you choose to eliminate them from your awareness.

Therefore, don't put your happiness on hold until all the circumstances in your life become perfect—or until your desires manifest. Do not take the position of waiting for your fortune to change before you become happy. Reverse-engineer your life by being happy now. Happiness begets more happiness— and attracts an avalanche of the positive conditions you want in your life.

If you are someone who wants to lose weight,

eliminate procrastination, become more productive, get rid of mental obsessions or addictions, resolve marital and personal relationship problems—and rise above any and all human dilemmas–the solution is as simple as consciously connecting to the field of all possibilities using the spiritual truths revealed in this book. Before long, you'll find yourself behaving in ways that would naturally cause those things to happen.

Surrender to prevalent circumstances in your life instead of trying to change them. When you're thankful for all things and infuse everything with love, you gain something that is exceedingly and abundantly more than you could ever ask, think or imagine.

> "Neither a lofty degree of intelligence nor imagination, nor both together, go to the making of genius. Love, love, love, that is the soul of genius."
> — Wolfgang Amadeus Mozart

If we were told we only have 10 minutes left before the end of the world, what would we do with that time? We would tell our loved ones that we love them. And yet in our busy workaday world, sometimes we allow days, weeks and months to go by without expressing our love to those whom we love. Do it today. Let love begin as a flame that you light within you. Love yourself first, and then spread that love beyond yourself and out into the world. Because at the end of our lives, we'll want to remember not how well we lived but how well we loved.

As I come to the end of this book, it is my wish that I've impressed upon you that when you apply the greatest manifestation principle of love to every aspect of your life, your desires have the greatest likelihood of manifesting. When your desires are motivated and nourished by love—and you stay connected to the energy field through love—your desires MUST manifest because love is the most powerful magnetic force in the universe that attracts miraculously wonderful things to you that are often greater than your desires.

But the greatest miracle, by far, is that as you become fully aware of love's presence within you, you'll discover the greatest joy of all—that love is its own reward. When you realize that your capacity to love comes from the divine presence within you, and that love is God's way of affording you a glimpse of his own unfathomable love, you'll know without a doubt that God's power is available to you every time you choose to love.

APPENDIX

How to Eliminate the Biggest Obstacles That Prevent You from Manifesting Your Heart's Desires

In the preceding chapters of this book, I've presented what I believe is the ultimate "blueprint" to manifesting your best life a certainty—instead of something merely hoped for.

However, I realize that there is still a long-standing question that most people ask with regards to manifestation: Why do some people manifest their heart's desires—but most don't?

That's because there are 4 major obstacles which keep them from manifesting successfully. Two of them were already mentioned in previous chapters, but they're worth summarizing here for easy reference.

Obstacle No. 1: Cellular Memories and Wrong Beliefs

Cellular memories are memories which have imprinted themselves in the cells (i.e., memories stored independently of the brain) as a result of life experiences. The phenomenon known as "cellular memory" is based on the theory that cells can store memories about sensations, taste, habits, aspects of someone's identity, and experiences—including traumatic experiences.

Substantial research evidence suggests that repressed anger, hate, resentment, and grief create cellular memories. Some of these memories—oftentimes from early childhood and beyond—give off destructive energy signals of fear, low self-worth, depression, sadness, anxiety, irritation, resentment, bitterness, and all the emotional states that are categorized as low-vibration destructive states, which are not the ideal springboard for manifesting.

Cellular memories are like tiny radio stations transmitting destructive frequencies (internal stress) within the body, and these are widely acknowledged as the cause of 95% of all diseases. The destruction they wield often goes unnoticed because people rarely associate diseases with the energetic disturbances caused by cellular memories.

Wrong beliefs are beliefs that are ingrained in our subconscious mind due to negative programming, dysfunctional family upbringing, and a host of other factors. They manifest themselves as internalized scripts that keep playing in one's subconscious. Examples of wrong beliefs are statements like "You're not good enough" or "Why are you so stupid?" or "You'll never amount to anything" or sometimes, they may be distorted interpretations of scripture, like "Money is the root of all evil", which is wrong since the correct scripture is "The love of money is the root of all evil".

Therefore, suppose you have the wrong belief that "Money is the root of all evil" in your subconscious mind—how would that affect your desire to manifest wealth in your life? Since your wrong belief is at cross-purposes with your desire, the desire has no chance to see fruition because it's being sabotaged by the wrong belief simmering under the surface. Many desires are arrested and never allowed to manifest into existence due to wrong beliefs.

Another example of how wrong beliefs can sabotage your manifestation progress: Suppose your desire was to win the lottery. But you have a wrong belief that people will steal from you or take advantage of you. Then the vision you hold in your mind of winning the lottery is accompanied by fear that people will be circling you like vultures, hitting you up for money, coaxing you into shady investment schemes—and you live in trepidation that you will become prey to criminals.

Do you see how wrong beliefs can sabotage your ability to manifest your desire?

It's also worth noting that wrong beliefs create stress in our autonomic nervous system, according to Dr. Bruce Lipton, a developmental biologist who was able to prove this in the laboratory. The emotional state that corresponds to stress is yet another destructive state that is not conducive to successful manifesting.

There are numerous modalities that could enable you to change or neutralize wrong beliefs—such as holographic repatterning, Emotional Freedom Technique (EFT), PSYCH-K, Inner Resonance Technologies (IRT) and Neurological Integration System (NIS), among many others.

The simple zero-cost method for neutralizing wrong beliefs without your having to undergo the aforementioned therapies—which may or may not work—is the Love's Pathway exercise. It neutralizes both harmful cellular memories and wrong beliefs, transmutes the low-vibration frequencies and elevates them to the level of love and above (500 to 600 Hz). One tool that could enhance your practice of Love's Pathway is an app called "Sublime Buzz™" (www.sublimebuzz.com).

Obstacle No. 2: False Desires

Socrates, the philosopher from ancient Greece who founded Western philosophy, once wrote that every man pursues only the good, but he doesn't know what REAL good is.

The same is true for desires. You might think you're pursing something good, but now is the time to examine them more closely.

Media—especially social media—influences individual beliefs, behaviors and attitudes more than we realize or care to admit. Influencers—both online and offline—shape what people desire, crave, and obsess over. Those desires tend to center around materialism and consumerism.

This may be why the average person—when asked to identify what they want to manifest into existence—choose wealth, worldly possessions and other frivolous playthings that promote self-centeredness or meaningless pursuits.

These are false desires—the kinds that are unlikely to manifest into existence. Or if they do happen to manifest, they would seldom bring you fulfillment or the feeling that you're living your best life.

If your desire is to have a million dollars, for instance, ask yourself the question: "Why do I want it?"

The moment you ask the question, your brain is compelled to answer—and the answer will likely reveal a deeper motive for your desire.

In order to pursue a desire that is real and not false, your desire must be nourished and motivated by love—not selfishness, not a need to impress people or incite their envy, and not hostile competition, one-upmanship, wrongful pride, exploitation of the weak, or other meaningless things.

But what if your desire is disguised as something you want for your family? Isn't that a worthy desire since it's motivated by love for one's family? To answer this question, one must determine whether the end result of our desire is simply a larger form of selfishness. For instance, suppose you desire to have a million dollars because you want to give your children more than you ever had when you were a child. This sounds noble, but when you peel away the layers of that desire down to its core, make sure your intended end result is not to make your kids superior to others, or give them bragging rights for owning or having something other kids don't. For that would make your desire a false one, and not one motivated by love. But if the end result you want is to provide your children with an education, for example, that will afford them better job opportunities when they grow up, enable them to prosper and build a comfortable life for themselves, then that is a real desire.

When examining your desires to find out if they are real or false, ask yourself the question: What purpose does my desire serve?

If the purpose of your desire is to elevate yourself at the expense of others, or to show to the world that you're something you're not—or any purpose other than love, you can change your desire to something that could produce worthy outcomes.

Pursuing false desires may be one reason why some of the wealthiest people in the world never feel as though they've achieved their heart's desires. Oftentimes, they feel empty, and the acquisition of more possessions and material things never satisfies them; they have an insatiable need for more that could never fill the void inside. One might ask, "Are they living their 'best life' then, if they're always in a state of lack, never feeling that they have enough?" I think not.

When you peel away the layers of your desire, you often discover that it's not what you really want. It was just your way of getting to your real desire—that of being loved, being whole, and being fulfilled.

So instead of pursuing false desires, hold in mind a benevolence and kindness for all creation, let go of wanting the things of the world, and let the universe bring you what you really need, based on the good intention you hold in mind. You already know at the deepest level of your being what you truly desire—so there's no need to focus on it. You simply connect to the energy field (the Divine Creative Consciousness of Love), which is God, and allow your heart's desires to manifest. (See page 52)

Obstacle No. 3: Failure to Be Guided by Spontaneous Right Action

True manifestation is a phenomenon that happens when people envision themselves as having a particular desired result—and ideal opportunities, people, resources, circumstances, events and situations that contribute to that desired result manifest themselves without any prompting. It requires no force to make it happen, but relies instead on the greatest manifestation principle, which is love. This doesn't mean that some action is not required—but that action is done in a natural, easy manner as a result of the principle of spontaneous right action. (See page 44)

The principle of Spontaneous Right Action means that when you reach a high level of consciousness —such as the levels of consciousness you arrive at when you connect to the energy field—the "right" actions required for the full manifestation of your desires reveal themselves to you. All you have to do is heed them and act upon those revelations that are intuitively derived.

If you fail to heed the promptings of spontaneous right action—or choose to ignore them in favor of ego-driven actions which utilize force—then you fail to employ the power of the greatest manifestation principle, which automatically produces action that is in harmony with nature and one's own good.

The key is to elevate the quality of your connection to the energy field. When you enter the state of being connected to the divine—of being love—the right action becomes self-evident, without requiring the ego to figure out what to do. Set the "right action" in motion as it occurs to you—and this will ensure the highest likelihood of success in manifesting your desires.

Obstacle No. 4: Perception

"He who is not contented with what he has, would not be contented with what he would like to have."
— Socrates

We all want to be happy. Yet, we often put our happiness on hold until all the circumstances in our life become perfect—or until our desires manifest. That is the surefire way of not manifesting your desires.

Happiness is not an emotion that is caused by people, events or circumstances. It is a state that we choose to create in ourselves, sometimes as a result of people, events and circumstances. We've been conditioned to rely on external things to make us happy, when in fact, we don't have to wait for them to happen to us in order to be happy. Since we already know that happiness is something we choose to create, based on how we represent circumstances to our own mind, it stands to reason that you can choose to create happiness anytime, without waiting for luck or good fortune to come around, or before your desires are manifested. (See page 111)

Ultimately, it is your own perception of your life, the

world and everything in it that can determine whether you have your best life or not.

Take a humble weed, for instance. Do you view it as beautiful or ugly?

Your perception of the weed is what you project onto the world. Essence is what the weed really is.

The reason you can't see the essence of things is because you project your judgmental perception on everything you see.

But if you choose to behold the stunning beauty, the sacredness, and the perfection in all living things—including a weed—then it is this perception of the world that becomes your *experience* of the world.

As discussed in Chapter 4, you'll know you've fully unmasked your true loving nature when you begin to see the world and everything in it as being beautiful. This means you've seen within yourself the beauty of who you are—the beauty of love. And you project onto the world what you see inside.

This elevated perception, then, is the profound concept which, when mastered, will provide you with the rarefied perspective of instantly having everything you desire—even before you manifest it into your life!

When you use the power of perception properly, you

begin to realize that you already have a life that is beautiful in every moment. It may not be your best life yet, but what you have at present is already awe-inspiring and wondrous.

Gratitude for what exists in your life at the present moment is the ultimate state of receptiveness—a state of trust and readiness to receive what the universe, divine intelligence, divine creative consciousness of love—God—has in store for you.

This brings us full circle back to the prime premise of quantum physics, which states: How you look at things affects what you *believe* you see.

Change the way you look at things, and the things you look at will change.

If you enjoyed this book, you may wish to …

√ Order copies to give away as gifts to friends and family by going to

http://www.GreatestManifestationPrinciple.com

Quantity discounts are available, as follows:

3 copies = 20% discount
4 to 11 copies = 30% discount
12 to 37 copies = 40%
38 or more copies = 50%

Note: If ordering online at www.GreatestManifestationPrinciple.com, quantity discounts are automatically calculated after you enter the quantity you're ordering.

√ Share your comments by sending e-mail to

Comments@GreatestManifestationPrinciple.com

Think-Outside-the-Book, Inc.
8465 W. Sahara Avenue, Ste 111-497
Summerlin, Nevada 89117
(323) 331-9316